How to sell short
and
perform other
wondrous feats

How to sell short
and
perform other
wondrous feats

CONRAD W. THOMAS

DOW JONES-IRWIN
Homewood, Illinois 60430

First Printing, August 1976

ISBN 0-87094-127-5
Library of Congress Catalog Card No. 76-13083

Printed in the United States of America

Preface

This book is written for investors who want to
do better than average in the stock market,
believe it is possible to do so, and seek a logical
method to perform this "wondrous feat."

The system described here—based on the use of
all available facts—applies not only to stocks but
to all kinds of securities, from stodgy bonds to
flighty options. The system applies to selling securities "short" as well as investing in them "long."
It is, in fact, a comprehensive system of portfolio
management, designed to help both private
investors and professional money managers out-
perform the market averages on a consistent basis.

There is a theory abroad today, spread by a
fervid cult of academics, which says that no one
can beat the market. Cited in support are innumer-
able statistical studies which show that the average
investor, especially the average professional money
manager, has failed to beat the market on a
consistent basis.

As one of those immutable laws of academe
puts it, "Enough research tends to support one's
own conclusions." How on earth can the average
investor be expected to beat the market average?
It's like expecting the car in the middle of a train
to go faster than the train itself.

Somehow the theorists have jumped from the
obvious fact that the average investor cannot out-
perform the market averages to the conclusion that
no one can do so—*and so it is futile even to try.*
Some theorists will concede, to be sure, that a
few investors have outperformed the market on

occasion. But, they explain, the winners are not consistent over long time periods; and in any case their numbers are too few to be of any statistical significance. In other words, their successes can be explained, not by skill, but by pure chance alone.

This book is for those who cannot accept this defeatist theory—those who realize that top achievement in the stock market, as in other fields of endeavor, is limited to the small minority who excel in what they are doing because of their superior method and application. Only a few, by definition, can excel—and they've got to be doing something different than all the losers and average performers.

So please, if you do become a successful investor with the help of this book, keep it quiet. We don't want everyone to get into the act; that might cut down on our own odds. Don't boast about your success to your friends or relatives, not even to your spouse. And when your broker asks, as he will sooner or later, "Hey, what's your secret?" reply, as humbly as you can, "Just lucky, I guess."

Oddly, every reader of this book should find comfort in the fact that very few buyers will actually put the system into practice, so that any real danger from competition can be safely ruled out. First, not everyone who buys the book will read it. Of those who do read it in whole or in part, only a certain number will really understand it. Of those who do understand it, only a tiny percentage will have both the means and the resolve to put the system into practice. And even some of that tiny percentage, unable to evade Murphy's Law, will find some way to do it wrong.

By applying reasonable odds to each of the above steps, the author has concluded that no more than a few score (perhaps only me and thee) will apply the method with great success—and that no two will do so in quite the same way.

Thus, although this book can make it possible for every reader to beat the market, because even partial success will do that, only a few—to repeat—will excel.

This book is a distillation and further development of the investment approaches described in our earlier volumes, *Hedgemanship: How to Make Money in Bear Markets, Bull Markets, and Chicken Markets While Confounding Professional Money Managers and Attracting a Better Class of Women* (1970) and *Risk and Opportunity: A New Approach to Stock Market Profits* (1974). Letters from appreciative and helpful readers never fail to give the author a lift. All correspondence regarding the current book should be directed to me, Box 49471, Los Angeles, CA 90049.

Conrad W. Thomas
West Los Angeles, California
July 1976

Contents

Chapter 1

Introduction

CHAPTER 1. INTRODUCTION

Although this book describes a comprehensive system of investment, much of it is concerned with short selling—a subject avoided by most financial writers, just as the practice of short selling is avoided by most investors.

Nearly all investors, in fact, not only have an ingrained fear of short selling, but are even unable to define it. Their fear and ignorance have not been dispelled to any appreciable degree by stock market professionals, including brokers and institutional money managers. These people have prejudices of their own, often reinforced by house rules which inhibit or prohibit short selling.

Moreover, various agencies of the United States government itself have long looked with suspicion on short selling. They make it somewhat more difficult to accomplish than ordinary investing, and tax any profits made by selling short with even greater enthusiasm.

No doubt, a lot of the bad odor associated with short selling can be traced to the days of the robber barons, when such disreputable practitioners as Jim Fisk, Jay Gould and Dan Drew made unforgivable displays of their ill-mannered successes.

In a later era, with the economy virtually paralyzed by the aftermath of the stock market excesses that climaxed in the Great Crash, President Franklin D. Roosevelt sponsored legislation to create the Securities and Exchange Commission (SEC), which was supposed to bring about a healthier and less crooked investment climate on Wall Street. To head the new agency, the presi-

dent appointed Joseph P. Kennedy, who was not
only the sire of a notable family of politicians
but also a prominent and successful short seller.
This appointment appeared to be a classic case of
picking a fox to watch over the chickens.

At any rate, reforms were certainly needed.
Some were passed then, and many more have
been passed since those dark days of the early
30s. Even today, though, many observers feel that
the SEC is a gutless enforcer. Indeed, the commission does seem to settle most violations of the
law by letting those charged promise to stop
doing what they shouldn't have been doing in the
first place—without admitting that they were
doing it.

Even when the culprits are convicted, the penal-
ties meted out seem mere wrist slaps. In one case in
point, certain employees of Merrill Lynch dis-
closed unfavorable inside information about
Douglas Aircraft to favored institutional investors,
who lost no time in selling their holdings in the
stock or in selling short on a massive scale.
Among those favored customers were the then-
popular hedge funds, which use short selling as a
fundamental part of their strategy.

Hedge funds such as those just mentioned have
added to the bad reputation of short selling
during recent years. The main reason is that they
have generally been so inept at it (unless, of
course, they had access to inside information, as
in the Merrill Lynch case).

During the great bull market of the 60s, which
peaked in December 1968, hedge funds prospered
beyond the wildest dreams of their partners
(most of the funds were private), simply because
they were riding long on the most volatile stocks

during a bull market, and were using top debt leverage besides. When the market slide started, they were caught with vulnerable long positions and no shorts at all. Then, instead of shifting swiftly to big short positions which would have been profitable, they liquidated their long positions slowly during the pitiless market decline, and went into cash. (The details of this gripping saga are related in our book *Hedgemanship.*)

The end result for most of the hedge funds was, of course, liquidation, along with eternal damnation by the greedy but somewhat naive moneybags who had entrusted their money to the glamorous new gunslingers. Even the few hedge funds that survived suffered massive losses of capital—not to mention reputation. Some have prospered since, notably in up markets.

Although our sample of chicanery and ineptitude has been small, the record is long, so it is small wonder that short selling is regarded by most people as an unmitigated evil. But that is simply not true. This book will demonstrate how selling securities short can and should be used to enhance the investment performance of both private investors and professional money managers. (We'll even get around to *defining* short selling in the next chapter.)

But one last statement before we leave this introductory chapter—an important message that we shall not shrink from repeating: Selling short and buying long are not all that different; the first is not perverted, the second normal. The criteria for arriving at buy, sell, and hold decisions—the very risk and opportunity measures demonstrated in this book—are the same for selling short as for buying long.

That is why this book—instead of concentrating on short selling as a scientist might concentrate on a rare bug species—demonstrates a *comprehensive* system of portfolio management, treating short selling as an integral part of a logical approach to profits in the stock market. In fact, the "other wondrous feats" promised in the title of this book stem from applying our risk and opportunity approach to buying long as well as selling short.

Chapter 2

What are we talking about?

CHAPTER 2. WHAT ARE WE
TALKING ABOUT?

Investment, to most people, means buying something in the expectation—not always realized—that it will go up in price over some future time period so that it can eventually be sold at a profit.

Buying, therefore, is usually the first step in the investment process, and any transaction is ultimately closed out—whether at a profit or at a loss—by:

Selling to someone else, who then becomes the investor.

Profit or *loss* on an investment is measured by the difference between the buying and selling prices, with costs and taxes, if any, either decreasing the profit or increasing the loss.

Buying "long" is exactly the same as *buying.* The word *long* is added in order to make clear the distinction between buying long and:

Selling short, which is the sale of something borrowed in the expectation—not always realized, either—that its price will go *down* over some future time period, so that the thing borrowed can be bought later at a lower price and replaced, thus affording a profit to the short seller.

A short sale of stock is made in the expectation that the price of the stock will decline. To illustrate: 100 shares of Burroughs are sold short at 90. If the stock declines to 60 and is bought, or "covered" (as the expression goes), at that price, the profit to the short seller is $3,000 (less the usual costs). If the price, on the contrary, goes up to 100, and the fearful short seller decides to cover there, he takes a loss of $1,000 (plus costs).

Both selling short and buying long involve two transactions, a purchase and a sale. The only difference between selling short and buying long is that the sequence of these two simple transactions is reversed for the short sale: first the sale, then the purchase (to replace the borrowed stock).

Just as the long buyer finally completes his transaction by selling (or leaves the task to his heirs), the short seller must—sooner or later—complete his transaction by buying the number of shares he sold short.

One difference between selling short and buying long should be noted: If any dividends are payable on the stock during the period in which it is borrowed, the lender quite reasonably expects to receive them. So who do you think pays him? Of course, the person who borrowed the stock to sell short. (The short seller can avoid this minor inconvenience by shorting stocks which pay no dividends; these are often better targets, anyway.) The company, of course, pays any dividends due, so the new owner of the stock gets them, just as though the stock he bought had not been sold short—he couldn't care less who the seller was. And when the borrowed shares are finally returned, they are not represented by the stock certificate that was borrowed but by an identical one—the lender couldn't care less about this either. In fact, the way things normally work, the lender doesn't even know that his stock has been borrowed by his broker.

We have the Securities and Exchange Commis-

sion to thank for another difference between
selling short and buying long: the "uptick" rule.
Short sales of listed securities can by law be made
only on the "uptick" or "zero-plus tick." This
means that the price at which a short sale is made
must be at least one eighth of a point higher (the
uptick) than the preceding sale of that stock, or
at the same price as the preceding sale if *that* was
higher than the preceding different price. The
uptick rule was dreamed up after the Great Crash,
and was designed to moderate the depressing
effect that concentrated short selling might otherwise have on a declining stock or market.

A "downtick" rule to moderate excessive
upward price movements (which have cost investors infinitely more than all the short selling in
history) would make a lot more sense than the
uptick rule. However, such a rule (never even
contemplated, of course) would be considered by
all upright citizens as immoral if not downright
ungodly.

The Internal Revenue Service takes credit for
still another difference between buying long and
selling short: It taxes more harshly any profits
made by the latter. Although profits made
on long positions held more than six months are
taxed as long-term capital gains, *all* profits from
short positions, no matter how long held, are
taxed at the higher short-term rate. There is only
one way to beat this rap: Don't short the stock
itself, but buy a put *option* and hold it for over
six months, then don't exercise the option but
sell it. An option is like any other piece of
property in that if purchase and sale take place in
the approved sequence, and the position is held

more than six months, any profit is taxed as a long-term gain.

We have written elsewhere about the morality of selling short (in *Hedgemanship* and in a *Barron's* article of November 2, 1970, "Primer for Shorts: How to Survive and Even Prosper in a Bear Market"). We won't repeat the argument here. Just take our word for it: Profits made from selling short are every bit as moral as those made from buying long—and may even be a bit sweeter.

Although short selling is still regarded almost universally as a tool of the Devil, it can, if properly used (like fire, another of his rumored tools), serve many useful purposes. Over and above the uses of short selling noted in Chapter 17, it can actually serve the public weal.

It has long been recognized that a substantial short position represents future demand for stocks, and therefore gives strong support to the market. The people now most active in short selling are floor members of the stock exchanges, especially the specialists, who are specifically *charged* with maintaining orderly markets in the stocks assigned to them. They do this by buying for their own accounts when public demand is slack, and by selling from their own accounts—or selling short—when public demand exceeds supply. One would suppose that these altruistic, self-sacrificing chaps would welcome all the help they could get from the public, particularly in the allegedly dangerous business of selling short.

Further, let's consider the individual investor and his role in the overall economy. If everyone ignores short selling and invests only long, then everyone is hurting at once when the stock market plunges—or everyone is delirious at the same time during bull markets. This state of affairs naturally leads to extremes in the economy itself. (We wonder why the president's Council of Economic Advisers doesn't go to work on this.) How much more stable the economy would be if half the people at any one time in any kind of market were short sellers and the other half were in longs. Then they could all take turns feeling sad and glad. (We must face the fact that only a very few people will learn to use risk and opportunity measures with the skill required to avoid melancholy in all kinds of markets.)

Now, if you have never made a short sale, we are going to tell you everything you need to know about making one—everything you need to know as far as your part in the process is concerned.

If you have good reason to believe that a particular stock is way overpriced and is due for a healthy correction on the downside—*forget* upticks and zero-plus ticks, *forget* where your broker borrows the stock, *forget* about whether your clergyman would approve. Simply call your broker and say: "Short Zombex [or whatever the stock is called] at 94 [if that's about where it is now], or as close to 94 as you can."

That's all there is to making a short sale.

Of course, you'd better use risk and opportunity measures to get some numbers on "way overpriced" and the "healthy correction" that's coming—and also to set appropriate price guidelines not only for making the short sale but also for covering it when the time for that comes.

Let your broker keep you informed of current margin requirements, both initial and maintenance. Margin deposit requirements for both long and short positions ease as prices move in the desired direction, and become more stringent if prices move too far in the opposite direction. Your broker can tell you for any stocks in your portfolio the prices at which he will make calls for more margin.

If this ghastly event ever happens to you, please reread this book—more carefully than the first time.

Chapter 3

Morgan's law: The market will fluctuate

CHAPTER 3. MORGAN'S LAW:
THE MARKET WILL FLUCTUATE

Back in the Dark Ages of Wall Street, a young financial reporter asked J. P. Morgan, the elder, "What is the stock market going to do, Mr. Morgan?" No doubt, the newsman was hoping for a hot tip—that staple of investment decision-making, then as now. He got no such thing.

"The market will fluctuate!" replied the great man.

Even today this oft-quoted remark is regarded by almost everyone as facetious, and certainly as of no practical use in the stock market.

The fact is that "Morgan's Law" (as we have called it in other writings) is very useful indeed, and must be the basis for any logical investment approach.

The only undeniably true prediction which can be made about any stock—be it blue chip or the rankest garbage—is that its price will fluctuate. Learned analysts can examine the company from top to bottom, calculate any number of financial ratios, estimate future sales and earnings, study the state of the industry and of the overall economy, evaluate the effect of international events on the company, ad infinitum—and still be uncertain about the future of the stock price. Of only one thing can they be *sure:* the price will fluctuate.

With this as the starting point, the next logical question is: *How much* will the price fluctuate?

In most cases, this question can be answered with a reasonable degree of assurance. We all know that security prices jump around with various degrees of animation. And we can predict that the prices of fixed-income securities, such as bonds, will fluctuate less than the prices of stocks, that the prices of stock options will fluctuate more than those of common stocks, and that the price of Polaroid, for example, will fluctuate more than that of American Telephone.

Such price fluctuations are ordinarily referred to as "volatility." We say: "Polaroid is much more volatile than American Tel." But *how much* more volatile?

THE BETA COEFFICIENT

Various financial services are now prepared to answer this question in a quantitative way. The standard against which relative volatilities are measured is some selected broad market index, such as the Dow, the New York Stock Exchange Composite Index, or Standard & Poor's 500. The measure is called the "beta coefficient," or simply the "beta." It is a measure of comovement with the market.

The beta concept was developed by "efficient market" theoreticians, and it is a part of their "capital asset pricing model," in which it applies to relative changes in the rate of return of a security as against that of the market, over and above some "risk-free" rate of return (such as the yield on Treasury bills). In this form, the concept is hard for nontheorists to understand and apply, and is of limited practical use even to those who claim to understand it.

As we have pointed out elsewhere, besides the several admittedly far-out assumptions underlying the theory (such as zero transaction costs), rate of return (appreciation plus dividends) is a variable figure that depends upon the theoretician's arbitrary choice of the time period used in a particular study, and also on the number of time periods used. Some studies go back 40 years and more, raising questions as to the relevance of such hoary data to today's prices. These studies' "rate of return" is, in fact, nobody's real rate of return, but merely a statistical convenience.

Much more useful, and at least as accurate, we believe, is the concept of simple price comovement with the market: the amount of price change a stock usually undergoes for a given move in the averages. We have called this the Poor Boy beta because of its ease of understanding and calculation.

To illustrate, let's say that the market, as measured by some average, moves up or down 1 percent, and that during the same time period the price of International Paper moves 2 percent in the same direction. The beta for IP, then, is 2. If, during the same time period, the price of Union Carbide changes by 1.5 percent, its Poor Boy beta is 1.5. By means of the Poor Boy beta, the volatility of any stock can be compared to that of all other stocks on a numerical basis.

This concept, and how to use it in selecting winners, will be developed in Chapter 14, "Swinging with the market."

THE PROFIT POTENTIAL
IN PRICE FLUCTUATIONS

Morgan had the key, although he did not choose to spell out the concept in detail for the reporter. The main potential for making money in the stock market lies in the magnitude and frequency of price changes.

This statement is true both for buying long and for selling short. The key to making money by investing long is buying low and selling high. The key to making money by selling short is selling (short) high and buying (covering) low.

Obvious, no doubt. Until we ask: "What is *high* and what is *low?*" These fuzzy terms can be defined very clearly by applying risk and opportunity measures, as we shall see.

WHAT ABOUT DIVIDENDS?

Although dividends can be obtained with much less effort than capital gains, they are of minor importance compared to the profit potential inherent in price fluctuations. However, in Chapter 5 we'll show how to calculate the effect of dividends and interest in cases where their effect may be appreciable.

Chapter 4

Defining risk and opportunity: The need for numbers

CHAPTER 4. DEFINING RISK
AND OPPORTUNITY: THE
NEED FOR NUMBERS

In the previous chapter we said that the main potential for making money in the stock market lies in the magnitude and frequency of price fluctuations. For buying long, the profit potential lies in the magnitude of the price difference between buying "low" and selling "high." And for selling short, the profit potential lies in the magnitude of the price difference between selling short "high" and covering "low."

In order to be useful in a logical system of investment, the words *magnitude, low,* and *high* must be quantified—that is, expressed in *numbers.* However, it is a perverse quality of human nature that people try their utmost to avoid the use of numbers, especially in stock selection and timing. (They prefer to restrict their arithmetic exertions to sports statistics or adding up profits, if any.) This fact helps to account for the popularity of books which promise easy riches from the stock market without having to bother with numbers.

Even professional money managers have not been noted for developing effective quantitative approaches for assessing the investment merits of stocks (and their results show it—especially over the long run). Instead of using some numerical scale as a guide to making investment decisions, money managers tend to rely on such "measures" as the hunch, the grabber (for those who must be "grabbed" in order to make up their minds), the gut-wrencher (for those who depend on "gut feeling"), and the pants-tingle (for the many who proudly "fly by the seat of the pants").

For all users of these indefinite measures to assess stocks, we offer—as a step toward quantification—the term *intuit*. The intuit (not to be confused with input) is defined as a unit of intuitive response to the receipt of information, often incorrect and always incomplete. The strength of the response is rated by the number of intuits aroused.

In *The Money Game*, Adam Smith quoted "Mister Johnson," who masterminded the Fidelity group of mutual funds during their glory days: "I know this is no science. It is an art. Now we have computers and all sorts of statistics, but the market is still the same and understanding the market is still no easier. It is personal intuition, sensing patterns of behavior. There is always something unknown, undiscerned."

An art, of course, is something one does without being able to explain how or why. Like Mister Johnson, most professional money managers are pleased to have whatever they are doing thought of as an art. The word does have a nice ring to it.

However, there is no consistent, logical way to compare the investment merits of securities at any given time without the use of some method of *quantifying* those merits—converting available information into numbers. The system we have devised for doing so is described in detail in the book *Risk and Opportunity*, and the aim of the present book is to make the system even more understandable and useful.

Only simple arithmetic is needed to calculate investment risk and opportunity, and their ratios. Anyone familiar with the elementary-school arithmetic symbols can make these calculations.

A hand or desk calculator can ease the pain that some may associate with arithmetic, but only pencil and paper are necessary. In the following chapters we shall demonstrate just how simple—and useful—the process is.

But first, let's define the things we'll be calculating, risk and opportunity.

Risk—in the usual investment process; that is, buying in the hope of selling later at a higher price—is exposure to the possibility of loss due to a *drop* in price.

Opportunity—for investing long—is the exact counterpart of risk: It is exposure to the possibility of gain due to a *rise* in price.

For selling short—selling borrowed stock in the hope of covering (buying) later at a lower price—the definitions of risk and opportunity are reversed.

Risk—for selling short—is exposure to the possibility of loss due to a *rise* in price.

Opportunity—for selling short—is exposure to the possibility of gain due to a *drop* in price.

(The effect of dividends will be explained in Chapter 5.)

It is important to keep in mind that the definitions for risk and opportunity, investing long and selling short, apply to *holding* positions at any current price as well as to *taking* positions at some initial price.

Now, let's see how these definitions can be made really useful by expressing them in *numbers*.

Chapter 5

Measuring risk and opportunity

CHAPTER 5. MEASURING RISK AND OPPORTUNITY

Both risk and opportunity can be measured by a combination of two factors, one depending on volatility, the other on current price.

MEASURING VOLATILITY

Price volatility is most easily and usefully reduced to a number by *range variability,* the difference between the high and the low divided by their average:

$$V = \frac{H - L}{A}$$

Volatility, V, contains both risk and opportunity. If the current price of a stock is near its projected low, buying opportunity is high and risk is low. On the other hand, if the current price is near the projected high, risk is high and opportunity is low.

When the current price of a stock is right at its projected low for any future time period selected, then risk is zero and opportunity is at a maximum. And, of course, if the current price is at its projected high, then opportunity is zero and risk is at a maximum.

All intermediate stages of risk and opportunity as the price of a stock fluctuates between its low and its high are measured by how far the current price is from some standard most conveniently, the average price.

MEASURING THE EFFECT
OF CURRENT PRICE

The second element of both risk and opportunity is called the "current price factor." This is twice the difference between the current price and the average price divided by the average:

$$C = 2\,\frac{P - A}{A}$$

In order to simplify both our calculations and our explanations, let us now fix in mind a few symbols that will be used throughout this book:

R = Risk.

O = Opportunity.

H = High price.

L = Low price.

A = Average of high and low = $\frac{1}{2}(H + L)$.

V = Volatility = range variability = $\dfrac{H - L}{A}$.

P = Current price.

C = Current price factor = $2\,\dfrac{P - A}{A}$.

MEASURING BUYING RISK

Risk is the combination of volatility plus the current price factor. In our symbols:

$$R = V + C = \frac{H - L}{A} + 2\,\frac{P - A}{A}$$

(For readers who may be interested, the derivation of the risk and opportunity formulas, with pictures, is given in our book *Risk and Opportunity*.)

The simplest explanation for the multiplier 2 in the current price factor is that the total range, $H - L$, covers *two times* the distance from the average price, A, to either the high, H, or the low, L. The current price factor, C, therefore requires a multiplier of 2 in order for risk to be zero when the current price equals the low, $P = L$. To demonstrate with elementary algebra:

$$R = 0 \quad \text{when} \quad P = L$$

$$R = \frac{H - L}{A} + 2 \, \frac{L - \frac{1}{2}(H + L)}{A} = 0$$

Simplifying:

$$H - L + 2L - H - L = 0$$

So all the terms cancel out, as they should.

MEASURING BUYING OPPORTUNITY

Opportunity, as we have said, is the counterpart of risk. For a given stock, the range of both risk and opportunity increases or decreases along with the stock's volatility; therefore, both are measured in part by the same volatility factor.

The current price factor, in contrast, must be different in algebraic sign for risk and opportunity, because a high current price means higher risk but lower opportunity, while a low current price means lower risk but higher opportunity.

Therefore, opportunity is equal to volatility *minus* the current price factor:

$$O = V - C = \frac{H - L}{A} - 2 \, \frac{P - A}{A}$$

To demonstrate again the need for the multiplier 2, opportunity is zero when the current price is at its projected high:

$$O = 0 \quad \text{when} \quad P = H$$

$$O = \frac{H - L}{A} - 2\frac{H - \frac{1}{2}(H + L)}{A} = 0$$

Simplifying:

$$H - L - 2H + H + L = 0$$

Again, the terms cancel out.

WHEN THE CURRENT PRICE IS ABOVE THE AVERAGE PRICE

A numerical example will make the formulas seem even simpler. Let's say that the current price of Polaroid is 35, its projected high for the coming year is 45, and its projected low 15.

The range, $H - L$, is $45 - 15$, or 30. The average price is $\frac{1}{2}(45 + 15)$, or 30. The volatility, V, is therefore 30/30, or 1.00. The difference between the current price and the average price is $35 - 30$, so the current price factor, C, is 2 times 5 divided by the average price, 30, or 0.33. Thus, risk:

$$R = V + C = 1.00 + 0.33 = 1.33$$

Is a risk of 1.33 good or bad? The answer comes with experience, comparison with the risk measurements of other stocks, and comparison with the stock's own opportunity.

$$O = V - C = 1.00 - 0.33 = 0.67$$

With a risk of 1.33 and an opportunity of 0.67 —an R/O ratio of 2—Polaroid seems a very poor buy at 35 (although it might be a fair short sale, with risk and opportunity values reversed).

It does seem obvious, in the light of the projected high and low, that Polaroid would not be a good buy at 35, and yet investors, even experienced money managers, *will* buy Polaroid at 35 and at *every* price between the high and low for any future time period. Even more remarkable, buying enthusiasm for Polaroid, as for other stocks, is commonly greatest at the high.

Thus, there would seem to be a value in making projections of future highs and lows simply in order to prepare the investor for bad news as well as good. Beyond this, the *quantification* of risk and opportunity—the reduction of these all-important qualities to simple numbers— allows the investor to make straightforward comparisons among various stocks, and thus to make logical decisions with respect to buying, selling, and holding.

It should be noted that a stock may be a good "hold" even though its current price is above the midpoint between its projected high and low, where its risk exceeds its opportunity. This matter will be discussed in later chapters.

WHEN THE CURRENT PRICE IS BELOW THE AVERAGE PRICE

In the example just studied, the current price of Polaroid, 35, was assumed to be above its projected average price, 30—midway between the high, 45, and the low, 15. It is instructive to go through the arithmetic involved in a case in which the current price is *below* the projected average.

Let's assume that Polaroid is selling at 20, rather than 35, and that the forecasts for the high and the low are the same as before. The average price is the same, 30, and so is the volatility, 1.00. But because the current price is different, the current price factor must be recalculated:

$$C = 2\,\frac{P-A}{A} = 2\,\frac{20-30}{30} = \frac{-20}{30} = -0.67$$

Note the minus sign. C is now negative because the average price is greater than the current price. Therefore, risk:

$$R = V + C = 1.00 + (-0.67) = 0.33$$

And opportunity:

$$O = V - C = 1.00 - (-0.67) = 1.00 + 0.67 = 1.67$$

(As every beginning math student quickly learns, subtracting a minus makes a plus.)

The O/R ratio is now 1.67/0.33, or 5, and Polaroid looks like a rather good buy at 20. But is it good enough? That depends on the selection criteria set by the investor. He may decide to wait until the price drops to the point where the O/R ratio is 10, or even 15. Or his decision to buy may be based on the risk level alone, perhaps 0.1. (Much more on this later.)

WHEN THE CURRENT PRICE EQUALS THE AVERAGE PRICE

To round out our Polaroid example, let's suppose that the stock is now selling at 30, exactly the same as its projected average price. The volatility, 1.00, remains the same as before because the projected high and low are unchanged. However, the current price factor, $C = (P - A)/A = (30 - 30)/30 = 0$. Therefore, both risk and opportunity are equal to the volatility, 1.00.

Whenever *any* stock is selling at its average price, risk and opportunity are evenly balanced, and the stock is neither a great buy nor a great sell, but it is, most likely, in the hold area where profits (and losses, regrettably) can accumulate. (More on this later, too.)

SELLING SHORT

The foregoing discussion applied to buying long. For selling short, the effect of current price is reversed, so $R = V - C$ and $O = V + C$. The reader may find it a worthwhile exercise to go back and recalculate the numerical examples, using now the formulas for selling short.

THE EFFECT OF DIVIDENDS
AND INTEREST

Although dividends are of minor importance in calculating the profit and loss potentials of most common stocks, dividends and interest can have an appreciable effect in the case of securities of relatively low volatility, such as bonds. In such cases, both the definitions of risk and opportunity and the formulas for calculating them are somewhat modified. We shall not have occasion to use these definitions and formulas again in this book, but, for the record, here they are.

For *buying long, risk* is defined as exposure to the possibility of loss resulting from a drop in price, lessened by the amount of the dividends (or interest) received.

$$R = \frac{H-L}{A} + 2\frac{P-A}{A} - \frac{2D}{A}$$

where D = Amount of dividends or interest.

For *buying long, opportunity* is exposure to the possibility of gain resulting from a rise in price, increased by the amount of the dividends received.

$$O = \frac{H-L}{A} - 2\frac{P-A}{A} + \frac{2D}{A}$$

For *selling short, risk* is exposure to the possibility of loss resulting from a rise in price, increased by the amount of the dividends payable.

$$R = \frac{H-L}{A} - 2\frac{P-A}{A} + \frac{2D}{A}$$

For *selling short, opportunity* is exposure to the possibility of gain resulting from a drop in price, lessened by the amount of the dividends payable.

$$O = \frac{H-L}{A} + 2\frac{P-A}{A} - \frac{2D}{A}$$

These formulas *should* be used whenever dividends or interest are appreciable in comparison to the volatility factor. The amount of dividends or interest is that expected over the probable period during which the long or short position will be held.

Chapter 6

Timing investment decisions

CHAPTER 6. TIMING
INVESTMENT DECISIONS

At the heart of any successful investment approach lies the need for effective buy, hold, and sell decisions—commonly referred to as "timing."

In using our system, these decisions are controlled by the criteria set by the individual investor or portfolio manager, and the most important of these criteria are risk, opportunity, and O/R and R/O ratios.

Because each timing decision comes down to the price at which we buy or sell, or the price range or limits we find acceptable for buying, selling, or holding, an essential step is to adapt the formulas already developed to tell us at what prices our criteria, whatever they may be, are met.

For example, we are considering purchase of a stock whose projected high and low are 100 and 40, respectively. The current price is near the average at the moment, so we resolve not to buy in until the risk drops to 0.1 or below. What will the price be then?

Substituting known amounts in the risk formula, and solving for P:

$$R = \frac{H - L}{A} + 2\,\frac{P - A}{A}$$

$$= \frac{100 - 40}{70} + 2\,\frac{P - 70}{70} = 0.1$$

$$60 + 2P - 140 = 7$$

$$P = 43.5$$

Therefore, we buy when the price drops to 43½ or below.

BUY OR SELL WHEN RISK IS GIVEN

For the general case, in which timing of any sort is determined by a given risk, the standard risk formula is solved for price, P. (Readers with no handle at all on algebra will have to take our word for the end formula, which *can* be solved with simple arithmetic.)

$$R = \frac{H-L}{\frac{1}{2}(H+L)} + 2\frac{P-\frac{1}{2}(H+L)}{\frac{1}{2}(H+L)}$$

$$H - L + 2P - H - L = \frac{1}{2}(H+L)R$$

$$\boxed{P = L + .25(H+L)R}$$

Let's try this on the numerical example above:

$$P = 40 + .25(140)0.1 = 40 + 3.5 = 43.5$$

BUY OR SELL WHEN OPPORTUNITY IS GIVEN

In this case, where opportunity is set by the investor for timing at any selected level, the opportunity formula is solved for price:

$$O = \frac{H-L}{\frac{1}{2}(H+L)} - 2\frac{P-\frac{1}{2}(H+L)}{\frac{1}{2}(H+L)}$$

$$H - L - 2P + H + L = \frac{1}{2}(H+L)O$$

$$\boxed{P = H - .25(H+L)O}$$

To illustrate numerically, assume a sale when opportunity drops to 0.2, with the projected high 100, the low 40.

$$P = 100 - .25(140)0.2 = 100 - 7 = 93$$

What this number is telling you is: Cash in your chips when the price hits 93, instead of trying to squeeze the last seven drops of blood from the dying bull. You should ride the Greater Fool theory only so far.

BUY OR SELL AT A GIVEN R/O OR O/R RATIO

$$\frac{O}{R} = \frac{\dfrac{H-L}{A} - 2\dfrac{P - \frac{1}{2}(H+L)}{A}}{\dfrac{H-L}{A} + 2\dfrac{P - \frac{1}{2}(H+L)}{A}}$$

$$\frac{O}{R} = \frac{H - L - 2P + H + L}{H - L + 2P - H - L}$$

$$\frac{O}{R}(2P - 2L) = 2H - 2P$$

$$P\left(\frac{O}{R}\right) - L\left(\frac{O}{R}\right) = H - P$$

$$P\left(\frac{O}{R} + 1\right) = H + L\left(\frac{O}{R}\right)$$

$$\boxed{P = \frac{H + L\left(\frac{O}{R}\right)}{\frac{O}{R} + 1}}$$

For a numerical example, let's look at the stock used above—high 100, low 40. We can assume any O/R ratio we wish. Let's say we demand an O/R of 5 before we'll buy. Substituting in the price formula:

$$P = \frac{100 + 40(5)}{5 + 1} = \frac{300}{6} = 50$$

Or let's insist on an O/R of 10:

$$P = \frac{100 + 40(10)}{10 + 1} = \frac{500}{11} = 45.5$$

So we see that, even using a very conservative O/R of 10 to 1, we can still buy in without fear at 45½, some 5½ points above the low forecast for the stock.

The concepts just illustrated as formulas will be presented pictorially in upcoming chapters which feature risk/opportunity diagrams and portfolio control models that are superimposed on R/O diagrams.

Chapter 7

Chartists, economists, and other seers

CHAPTER 7. CHARTISTS, ECONOMISTS, AND OTHER SEERS

Before we introduce the risk/opportunity, or *R/O*, diagram—a most useful way to visualize our system—let's touch briefly on some alternative visual aids, as well as on two widely used approaches to decision-making in the stock market.

It is all very well to calculate values of risk and opportunity, supply and demand, profit and loss, and the relation of population growth to the consumption of zonkers, but the human mind boggles when confronted with too many numbers. That is why man, as a prop to his limited brain capacity, has invented diagrams, graphs, and charts of various sorts.

For example, the pie chart (a most appropriately named device) is the favorite of government economists who try to explain where the tax dollar comes from, and where it goes. The pie slices are far easier to understand than a series of figures.

Charts, like numbers, can be used to lull or deceive, as well as to enlighten. Examples can be found in the annual reports of some corporations which support their claims of uninterrupted growth by resorting to rather odd interpretations of what constitute generally accepted accounting principles.

Other charts are based on fact, but their interpretation may depend more on necromancy than on science. These are the charts of the so-called technical stock analysts—popularly known as "chartists." Our comparison of charting with necromancy—which is the art of revealing the future by pretended communication with the spirits of the dead—is one of the few statements we make with which "random walk" economic theorists will agree, because they too believe that no amount of study of past price movements is of any help whatever in predicting future prices.

Nevertheless, charting is a widely practiced art, and no major institutional investor, including banks and insurance companies, feels safe without its own in-house necromancer. This is somewhat like not believing in God, but praying on occasion anyway just to be on the safe side.

For our part, we think that the one valid concept of technical analysis is its belief in the existence of trends—provided that: (a) the trends are based on fundamentals, and (b) it is realized that every trend must end, and then undergo a reversal. A trend, like a train, may be a good thing to ride as long as its destination is known.

As for the rest of charting—replete with such anthropomorphic jargon as "head and shoulders" and "double bottoms"—it would seem appropriate to put as much faith in this monster as one would in the Abominable Snowman. (Of course, we have our domestic version of the Tibetan phenomenon—the Abdominal Snowman. He's the artist who runs those portfolios largely by "gut feeling" and obscures his artful dodges with what used to be known as a snow job.)

Economists, especially those involved with investment theory, never tire of belittling the chartists, but one thing must be said for the chartists vis-à-vis the economists. The chartists never fail to use *numbers* on their charts: price, volume, support and resistance levels, and so on.

Economists, in contrast, generally prefer not to put any numbers on their charts, although they will happily draw legions of curves showing the relationship between risk and reward, and between the supply and demand of just about anything. Examples, with no numbers to detract from their charm, can be found in any economics textbook. Of course, some economists are in positions where they are forced to make predictions that can only be expressed in numbers: forecasts of the gross national product, for example, which everyone from the president on down expects.

Our thoughts about economists are not all negative. We do feel about them, however, much as we do about psychiatrists. Both work in areas that are very important to people, and both can make good diagnoses of what is wrong. The problems arise when they try to apply their cures. For years, no president has felt safe without his own panel of economic advisers, and some of the cures these panels have tried have resulted in trauma on a national scale. (Remember all those imposed economic "phases" of the Nixon years?)

For investors who seek the assistance of economists in making financial decisions—and all big money managers do so—"econometric models" have been devised which attempt to correlate stock market price changes with numerous economic factors. Sometimes these models seem to work quite well; on other occasions they fail. One must conclude that they are not reliable guides to the stock market. Astrologers, some of whom are stock market advisers, are right part of the time too.

One problem faced by investors who try to use

standard economic indicators, such as those issued periodically by the U.S. Department of Commerce, is that the stock market itself is one of the so-called leading indicators of the general economy. By the time the economy arrives at some specific point, the stock market is off and running somewhere else.

This short chapter may not enhance our reputation as either "the curse of the chartists" or "the economists' friend," but we hope that the discussion of charts and other pictures will help ease the reader into the next chapter—in which we introduce our own cherished risk/opportunity diagram.

Chapter 8

Risk and opportunity in practice and picture

CHAPTER 8. RISK AND OPPORTUNITY IN PRACTICE AND PICTURE

In earlier chapters we defined investment risk and opportunity, developed some simple formulas for their measurement, and illustrated their use with a few numerical examples. Now let's examine some other examples showing application of the measures in more detail, while introducing the risk/opportunity diagram as an aid to visualizing the measures and their uses.

For our first example, let's assume that after studying all the available information about a certain security—call it Stock A—we estimate that during the coming year its price will drop to a low of 60 and rise to a high of 100. Although we don't know just when during the year the high or the low will occur, or even which will occur first, we can calculate risk and opportunity at the start of the period.

With the projected high and low in hand, all we need to know now is the current price, which we get from the latest quotation in the financial pages of the newspaper, or from our broker's electronic gadgetry. Let's say the current price is $84 a share.

Using our formulas, we determine that risk, $R = V + C = (100 - 60)/80 + 2(84 - 80)/80 = 0.50 + 0.10 = 0.60$. Opportunity, $O = V - C = 0.50 - 0.10 = 0.40$. These values are plotted as a single dot in Figure 8-1.

This is called the risk/opportunity, or R/O, diagram. The vertical axis measures the amount of risk in buying into or holding a long position in a

Figure 8-1:   One stock plotted

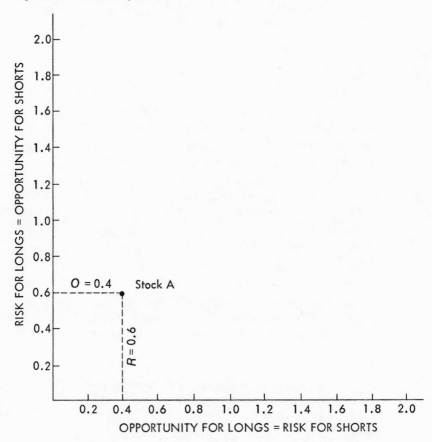

given stock at its current price. This "risk for longs" is always exactly equal to the "opportunity for shorts"–the opportunity in taking or holding a short position in the same stock at its current price. The horizontal axis measures "opportunity for longs" and its exact equal, "risk for shorts." A single dot thus defines risk and opportunity for both buying long and selling short at the current price.

Returning to our example, both the numbers and the diagram tell us that risk is greater than opportunity at the current price of 84. Therefore, this is no time to buy, because the price is due for a greater drop than rise—meaning that better buying opportunities will be available during the year.

Neither is Stock A a great selling—or short selling—opportunity at price 84, because of the substantial rise predicted into the 100 area.

If Stock A is now in the portfolio, it can probably be rated as a good "hold" until the selling criteria (higher risk, lower opportunity) are met.

However, a good reason for selling Stock A right now might be to put the money into another stock showing much higher opportunity along with lower risk. Such an alternative might well be Stock B (high 60, low 40, current price 45; therefore, risk 0.20 and opportunity 0.60).

The relative investment merits of Stocks A and B are made even more obvious by plotting their risk and opportunity values together, as in Figure 8-2. The investor or portfolio manager faced with the narrow choice of investing in either A or B would have little hesitation in making his decision in favor of B (provided, of course, that the stocks are of comparable investment quality).

The problem of comparing the investment merits of stocks naturally increases in complexity along with the number of stocks under consideration. This fact is illustrated by the addition of

Figure 8-2:   Two stocks compared

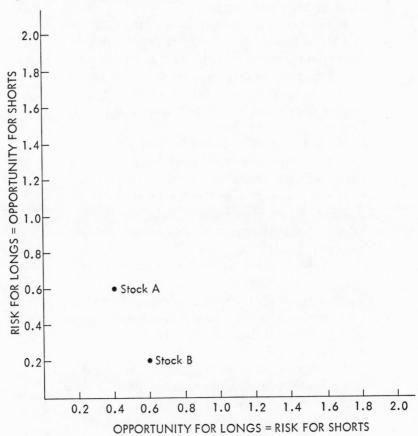

only three more stocks, C, D, and E, to the *R/O* diagram (Figure 8-3).

Stock B is still a better buy than Stock A, of course, but Stocks C, D, and E all show greater opportunity than does B. Offsetting this to some extent at least are the higher risk measures of C, D, and E. Stock E is even higher in risk than

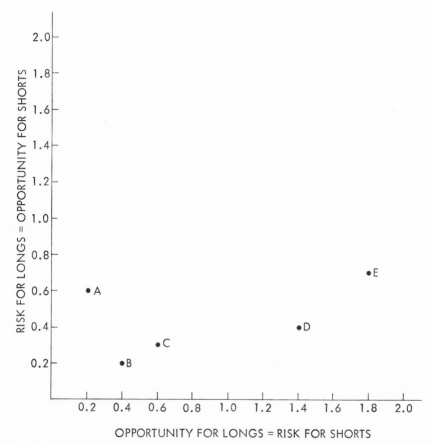

Figure 8-3:   Five stocks compared

Stock A. How do the five stocks now rate for
buy, hold, and sell?

Obviously, with even as few as five stocks,
some system is needed in making finer distinc-
tions among stocks. This lesson becomes even
more obvious when the field widens to 30 (Figure
8-4) or, worse, a few hundred stocks—the number

Figure 8-4: Thirty stocks compared

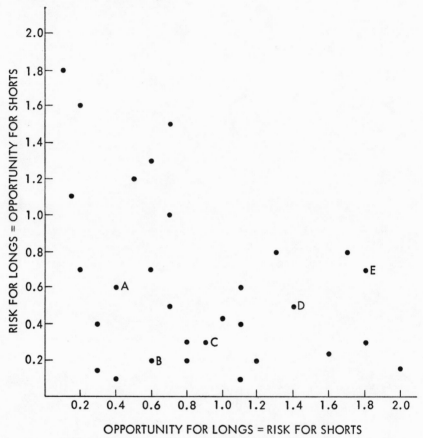

OPPORTUNITY FOR LONGS = RISK FOR SHORTS

on which most institutional investors try to keep tabs.

These big investors—banks, insurance companies, foundations, pension and mutual funds—can best use the *R/O* diagrams by showing only a limited number of stocks on each diagram—and by using such breakdowns as major holdings, industry groups, and so on. For overall compari-

sons of large numbers of stocks, computer print-
outs are recommended, with rankings from best
to worst based variously on risk, opportunity,
O/R ratio, volatility, profit and loss potentials,
investment quality, industry ratings, and whatever
other criteria are set by the organization itself.

The use of R/O diagrams and their computer
counterparts to assure that buy, hold, and sell
decisions are made on a logical and unemotional
basis will be demonstrated in later chapters. The
chapter "Control Models" will show how situations as seemingly complicated as the one in
Figure 8-4 can be clarified quite simply.

However, to illustrate in a simpler framework
some of the basic factors which enter into the
decision process, let's return to the small group
of five stocks in Figure 8-3.

We've already decided that Stock A is not a
good buy because its risk exceeds its opportunity
at this point—although it may be a good hold if
it is already in the portfolio, because it still has
considerable appreciation potential. Its price
could also retreat before advancing again, so it
might be prudent to sell now and take whatever
profit can be realized.

Let's say we bought Stock A when its risk was
only 0.1. According to our formula, the price was
then $P = L + .25(H + L)R = 60 + .25(160)0.1 = 64$.
The price is now 84, so we could realize a nice
profit of 20 points, for a percentage gain of 31.

But if our study of the fundamentals shows us
no reason why the stock should not approach
closer to its projected high of 100, we could well
decide to adhere to our original decision to hold
the stock until opportunity drops to 0.2. At that
point, the price will be $P = H - .25(H + L)O =$

$100 - .25(160)0.2 = 92$, still well below the projected high of 100. Profit is now 28, a gain of 44 percent.

Would 44 percent at this time be better than the 31 percent that could have been realized by selling out earlier at 84? Not necessarily. Not, for example, if it required four months to realize the 44 percent, while the 31 percent could have been taken after only two months. In all investment decision-making, we can never lose sight of the time value of money. Transaction costs and holding period (for tax considerations) may also be important in this type of situation.

Nonetheless, in most cases it is wise to adhere to our original timing criteria unless persuasive new information warrants changing those criteria.

Stocks B, C, and D at current prices represent progressively greater opportunity, along with increasing risk. All seem at first glance to be fairly good buys, because in each case opportunity is far greater than risk. But which is the *best* buy? Again, the answer depends on the criteria selected.

On the basis of relative opportunity and risk, Stock D, with an *O/R* ratio of 3.5, is the best buy, followed by B and C (both 3.0), then E (2.6).

However, if the maximum risk has been set at 0.2 or below, then B is the only stock able to qualify. If the minimum opportunity for purchase is 1.0, then only D and E qualify.

A ban on excessive volatility (above 0.8, say) would rule out both D and E. Gain potential, the possible profit to be realized between the current price and the selling price under whatever criteria are determined, could well be another constraint.

All of these problems, which may seem quite complicated when considered item by item, are greatly simplified by the portfolio control models that will be demonstrated later. As we shall see, these models are just as useful for short selling as they are for investing in the long, or conventional, manner.

Chapter 9

More on the risk/opportunity diagram

CHAPTER 9. MORE ON THE RISK/OPPORTUNITY DIAGRAM

In the preceding chapter we introduced the risk/opportunity diagram as a visual means of illustrating the investment merits of some hypothetical stocks. Now let's look at the basic R/O diagram in order to understand better some of the fundamental relationships it shows.

VOLATILITY

A volatility line is one showing the path traversed by the risk and opportunity values of a stock over a given period of time as the price of the stock fluctuates (with any number of changes in direction) in moving between its high and its low.

Certain stocks seem to traverse more or less the same volatility line during one cycle after another. Others make appreciable shifts because of unusual events affecting the company concerned, or because of events rumored to be happening or upcoming, or because of manipulation of one kind or another (it can still happen). However, even in cases where the shifts are "appreciable," the stocks will generally remain within some range of volatility which can be characterized roughly as "very low," "low," "medium," "high," or "very high."

As the R/O diagram (Figure 9-1) shows, volatility increases outward from the origin, where it is zero. Volatility, V, is measured by the difference between the high and the low divided by their average, so that a stock fluctuating in price

Figure 9-1: Basic risk/opportunity diagram

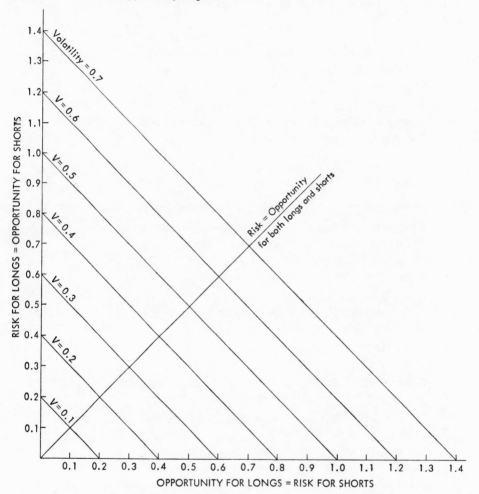

between 125 and 75 would traverse the $V = 0.5$ line on the diagram, while a tamer issue moving between 105 and 95 would be confined to the $V = 0.1$ line.

Volatility, as we know, contains both risk of

loss and opportunity for gain; exactly how much of each depends on the current price. The maximum potentials for both gain and loss increase along with volatility. The stock with a volatility of 0.5 has a gain potential of 66.7 percent if bought at its low and sold at its high—an extremely unlikely happenstance. The stock with a volatility of 0.1 has a maximum gain potential of only 10.5 percent if bought at its low and sold at its high.

Thus, low volatility can be a limiting factor for aggressive portfolios, just as high volatility can be a constraint on conservative portfolios. When limiting volatility criteria are adopted, the R/O diagram tells at a glance which stocks qualify and which are beyond the pale.

Note that the values of the volatility lines, which run at 45-degree angles between the vertical and horizontal axes, are exactly one half of the terminal risk and opportunity values—a state of affairs made inevitable, we suspect, by the formulas themselves.

Thus, the risk or opportunity of a stock with a volatility of 0.3, for example, can't possibly be greater than 0.6.

BUYING LONG AND SELLING SHORT

The risk/opportunity diagram shows that buying long is the mirror image of selling short. As prices wax, risk increases for buying and decreases for selling short; as prices wane, opportunity increases for buying and decreases for selling short.

By quantifying risk and opportunity, and by

setting timing criteria based on these measures, the investor can systematically "buy low and sell high" and sell short high and cover low.

The risk formula for buying long is the same as the opportunity formula for selling short: $V + C$. The opportunity formula for buying long is the same as the risk formula for selling short: $V - C$. Therefore, the vertical axis of the R/O diagram reads "Risk for longs = opportunity for shorts," and the horizontal axis reads "Opportunity for longs = risk for shorts."

Selling short should not be considered, as it commonly is, a bastard member of the investment family, but a legitimate brother of the favorite son—buying long. There is no real reason not to honor—and employ—them as equals.

THE RISK-EQUALS-OPPORTUNITY LINE

Running from the origin of the R/O diagram upward to the right at a 45-degree angle is the line showing where risk and opportunity are at a standoff. Risk is equal to opportunity, of course, whenever the current price is equal to the price midway between the projected high and low for any stock—the average price—because the current price factor is then equal to zero, and both risk and opportunity are therefore equal to the volatility.

Stocks whose current prices place them on or near the $R = O$ line are generally in a hold area; when stocks move away from that line, our surveillance of them must intensify, for timing action usually takes place near the extremes. How to use the volatility line as an action trap is described next.

Chapter 10

Trapping the wild security

CHAPTER 10. TRAPPING THE WILD SECURITY

In obedience to Morgan's Law, the market will fluctuate. Because "the market" is really a large, completely diversified portfolio, its fluctuations are always quite minor in comparison to the fluctuations of most of the individual stocks which together make up what we call "the market."

As we have seen, in the price fluctuations of stocks lie both risk and opportunity, and the possibilities for both increase along with the amount of fluctuation. Individual securities vary over wide ranges in their tendencies to fluctuate, but in many cases the degree of fluctuation remains relatively constant for successive periods; or it may change in a rather orderly or even predictable pattern. For example, the price range of a hot new glamor stock may decline rather steadily as the glamor wears off and investor expectations settle down.

Most stocks, especially those we term "cyclical" (and that includes just about all of them over one time cycle or another), have more or less characteristic degrees of price fluctuation, which we call volatility. We have no hesitancy in declaring, for example, that U.S. Steel is more volatile than American Telephone, or that United Technologies is more volatile than U.S. Steel.

Every security has, most of the time, a characteristic price volatility. As we have learned, this volatility can be measured by range variability, the difference between the high and the low divided by their average. This is the factor, V, which forms such an important part of our risk and opportunity measures.

On the risk/opportunity diagram, explored in the preceding chapter, the characteristic volatility of each stock is represented by a single diagonal line running between the vertical and horizontal axes. In a very practical sense, this line is a *trap* for the security it represents—a trap which makes it possible for the investor to capture and tame the security, no matter how wild it may be.

Let's illustrate with a practical example. Our study of all available information about Texaco, say, leads us to forecast its high for the year ahead at 30 and its low at 20. Volatility, V, is therefore $(H - L)/A = (30 - 20)/25 = 0.40$.

Texaco is now trapped on its volatility line, as shown in Figure 10-1. It can be compared to an ant crawling up and down a wire or (if you prefer a more formidable figure) a lion pacing up and down a long and very narrow alley. Neither ant nor lion can move left or right of its prescribed path, or go beyond its end limits.

Whether we think of it as insect or beast, what is actually trapped is price, and along with price all possible values of risk and opportunity along the volatility line, which in this case is equal to 0.40.

Table 10-1 shows the range of values for risk and opportunity for all round-dollar prices from 20 to 30, which are also represented graphically on the R/O diagram in Figure 10-1.

Although we have now confined the price movement of Texaco for the year ahead, confident that at one time (perhaps more) it will hit a low of 20, and that at another time (perhaps more) it will hit a high of 30, we cannot predict with any degree of certainty which will occur first, nor can we say much about the ups and downs that are bound to occur in between.

Figure 10-1:   Volatility trap for Texaco

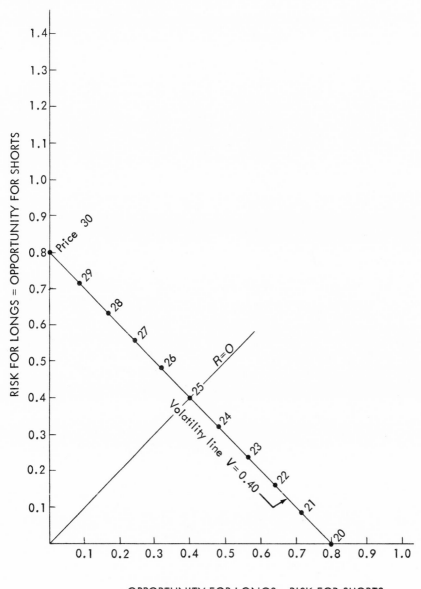

Table 10-1: Risk and opportunity values for Texaco over price range

Price	Current Price Factor *	Risk	Opportunity
20	−0.40	0.00	0.80
21	−0.32	0.08	0.72
22	−0.24	0.16	0.64
23	−0.16	0.24	0.56
24	−0.08	0.32	0.48
25	0.00	0.40	0.40
26	+0.08	0.48	0.32
27	+0.16	0.56	0.24
28	+0.24	0.64	0.16
29	+0.32	0.72	0.08
30	+0.40	0.80	0.00

*The algebraic signs are for calculating risk; they are reversed in calculating opportunity.

Nonetheless, our prey is trapped, and all we need is patience to achieve our ends.

Let's assume that at the start of the year the price of Texaco is 25. Risk and opportunity are equal (at 0.40), so the stock is neither a good buy nor a good short sale. So we wait, deciding not to buy until the price drops to a point where risk is 0.1 or less and opportunity is at least 0.7. At the same time, because we realize that the high might well be reached before the low, we decide to sell short if the risk of doing so falls to 0.1 or below and the opportunity rises to at least 0.7.

Now we merely have to be patient and track the price. No matter how wild the gyrations in between may be, the risk and opportunity values will cover the predicted ranges, and when the criteria at one end or the other of our narrow trap are met, we'll take action, either buying at the low-price end of the trap (at 21, say) or selling short at the high-price end (at 29).

Naturally, risk and opportunity criteria are also set for selling out a purchase and for covering a short sale when our prey is caught in either of the opposite ends of the volatility trap.

WHAT CAN GO WRONG?

Well, for one thing, if our estimates of the future high and low are way off base, our trap—instead of being a narrow line positioned just where we want it—may actually lie to the left or right, and its upper or lower limits may vary. Fortunately, as we shall see in later chapters, the prediction of precise highs and lows is not necessary. The method is still effective even though quite sizable errors are made in forecasting. Chapter 15 studies the consequences of errors in forecasting, and demonstrates that the system is still effective in spite of them; within limits, of course. Still, the worst that can happen is that criteria might be set so tight that some opportunities are *missed*.

Another thing that can happen to investors who buy only long and never sell short is that the predicted high will occur *before* the low, so that no buying action will be taken—another opportunity missed, but no blood spilled.

It cannot be stressed enough that the whole system is dynamic—that new predictions must be made whenever new information warrants them. Thus, if Texaco is bought at 21 early in the year, we need not necessarily sell it when it reaches 29 if, for example, increased earnings have been predicted by that time. Let's say that our new information at midyear leads us to predict a new price range of 27 to 40½. Our volatility trapline would remain the same (0.40), but the price range of Figure 10-1 would read from 27 to 40½ instead of from 20 to 40.

In similar fashion, stocks experiencing a long-term rising trend can be held for long periods of time (but don't ever be lulled into thinking you've found a "one-decision" stock). Likewise, short positions can be held for long periods of time in stocks suffering long-term downtrends.

To take full advantage of such long-term trends, it may be necessary to shift our traps from time to time in order to take new conditions into account, something any good trapper would do.

Chapter 11

Tracking a company

CHAPTER 11. TRACKING
A COMPANY

In order to study further how the risk and opportunity approach can be applied, let's follow the price action over a one-year period of a hypothetical stock we'll call Zombex. Zombex is a medium-sized manufacturing company with fairly steady earnings on an annual basis, but occasional marked variations from quarter to quarter.

Over the past few years its price volatility, as measured by range variability, has averaged about 0.35, and consideration of all available fundamental factors yields no reason to suppose that overall volatility in the year ahead will vary much from that figure, although rather sharp price changes may occur during the year. On the basis of the same fundamentals, we predict a price range of 33 to 47. A volatility of 0.35 is rather moderate compared to that of most of the 30 stocks making up the Dow Jones Industrial Index, as we'll see in Chapter 16.

Nevertheless, a volatility of 0.35, which means that the stock's price will fluctuate 35 percent around its average price, represents a fairly attractive profit potential for both buying long and selling short—provided that our predictions are not too far off the mark, and provided also that we make use of an effective plan for timing our moves.

TRACKING THE COMPANY AS A
LONG-BUY POSSIBILITY

Let's consider first our course of action if we decide to buy in at a low price in anticipation of a price rise. We'll be conservative, deciding in advance not to buy unless risk is 0.1 or lower, and opportunity at least 0.6.

Figure 11-1 shows that these conditions are met when the stock's price is 35 or below.

Figure 11-1:   Tracking as price changes

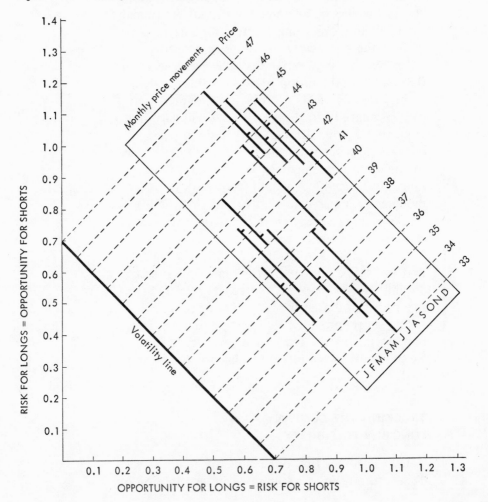

Also, we decide to play it close to the chest, selling out when risk reaches 0.5 or opportunity drops to 0.2. Figure 11-1 also shows that these selling conditions will be satisfied when the price rises to 43.

Buying at 35 and selling at 43 would mean a profit of $8 a share—a return of 23 percent, plus dividends. This is not a bad return considering the moderate volatility of the stock and the conservative criteria for buy and sell timing. It's not a bad return even if it takes a full year of price action. Chances are that it will take less than a year.

Having set our rules for decision-making, we now track the price action of Zombex. At the start of the year, as Figure 11-1 indicates, its price is 37. Risk 0.2, opportunity 0.5. Not bad, but not good enough for us.

During January the price drops as low as 36. Risk 0.15, opportunity 0.55. Better, but still not good enough.

Later in January the price rises to 39½, and we can't help wondering whether we've missed the boat. This feeling increases as the price hits 41½ in February and 43 in March. However, March prices dip to 40 and close at 40½; and April sees a further decline to 36½, about where the price was at the start of the year.

April prices continue their decline into May, and we buy in at 35. Although we have predicted a low of 33, which represents an even better buying opportunity, we realize that it may never be reached because our predictive powers are not perfect—nor need they be to achieve success.

But sure enough, June sees a further drop to 33, and the price might go even lower if we have overestimated the low. But even if it does so, we must stick to our guns if no new information has caused us to alter our fundamental predictions.

We are assuming in this hypothetical example that no basic changes occur during the year under study, but in practice such changes can occur, so continuous monitoring is the key to success in application of the method. For example, quarterly earnings reports and estimates of future earnings, if at variance with the figures that have been used to predict future highs and lows, will necessitate revision of those calculations. Thus, the method involves continuous updating, always looking ahead a year, say, from any point in time—rather than making forecasts for the year ahead and holding to them as one would to holy writ until the year expires.

Returning to our example: June is indeed the turnaround month, followed by substantial rises in July and August. Toward the end of August our predetermined selling price of 43 is reached, and we act on it even though we have predicted a further rise to 47.

Thus, we have captured a profit of 23 percent in about three months—on a not unusual price move in the stock market—for an annualized rate of return of about 92 percent. And all under the measurably conservative criteria we have set.

Now let's suppose that we choose to be even more conservative, still buying in at 35, but selling just as soon as risk rises to equal opportunity. Figure 11-1 shows that the risk/opportunity ratio is 1 when the price is 40, midway between the low and the high. This price is reached early in August. The gain of $5 a share represents a yield of 14 percent in less than three months. Minus costs, as usual.

The chart of price movements is representative but entirely hypothetical; the possible variations are infinite in number. However, in order to profit from the inevitable fluctuation in prices, only one condition must be realized: The favorable selling price must occur later than the buying price. (Not even this condition is necessary if the investor is willing to sell short as well as buy long.)

If, during the year, the price trend is downward, so that the high occurs before the low, no long position would be taken. Thus, although no gain would be realized, no loss would be suffered either.

TRACKING THE COMPANY AS A SHORT-SALE POSSIBILITY

In order to profit by selling short, one must take a short position at a relatively high price and cover it later at a low price. A generally declining price movement is therefore required during at least a part of the period.

The price chart of Zombex for the year illustrated in Figure 11-1 shows declines but no really great opportunities for short selling, if conservative criteria are adopted. It is true that the decline from the March high (43) to the July low (33) amounts to $10 a share—a possible gain of 23 percent in a few months. However, even if the high of 43 could be pinpointed, the risk in taking a short position at that price would be 0.2, along with an opportunity of 0.5. (Risk and opportunity for short selling, as we keep reminding ourselves, are the reverse of those for long buying.) Such odds are not bad, but it is wiser to wait for still better odds—opportunity of 0.6, say, and risk of only 0.1—criteria which are met at a price of 45.

This price is available in August, and during December the price falls as low as 40. At 40, risk and opportunity are equal at 0.35—which might satisfy very conservative guidelines for covering a short sale. However, the goal for price depreciation would probably be greater, so an assessment of the value of Zombex as a short sale at 45 would have to be made on the basis of predictions of price behavior in the several months that lie ahead. Such a basis for new forecasts would normally become available long before the final months depicted in Figure 11-1. This theme will be developed in the following chapter.

Chapter 12

More tracking and short selling

CHAPTER 12. MORE TRACKING
AND SHORT SELLING

In order to calculate useful values of risk and
opportunity as bases for investment decision-
making, it is necessary to forecast probable highs
and lows for at least several months in the future.
One year is a convenient period to use, with
reviews and revisions at least quarterly as new
information becomes available.

In the example detailed in the previous chapter,
we noted that in the month of September, when
Zombex hit its predicted high, it might have been
a good candidate for selling short. It was not
possible to say for sure whether or not it was
until forecasts were made for several months into
the future.

Many cyclical stocks come close to repeating
their highs and their lows cycle after cycle; that,
of course, is why they are called cyclical. Such
stocks are not hard to find, especially in essen-
tially sideways markets, which can continue year
after year.

Let's assume, after studying all available fundamentals, that Zombex will continue its cyclicity
at least into the year ahead, and that its high (47)
and low (33) will be the same as in the past year.
It need not hit those precise figures for our
system to be effective, because our buy, hold,
and sell criteria allow for some margin of error.

If the price of Zombex is going to fall again to
somewhere near its previous low of 33, then
September is a good time to take a short position
in the stock.

Let's say our criteria for selling short and
covering are the same as those used for trading

long in the preceding chapter; namely, sell short when opportunity is at least 0.6 and risk no more than 0.1, and cover (buy) when opportunity drops to 0.2 and risk rises to 0.5. Risk and opportunity values for selling short, we remember, are the reverse of those for buying long.

Having fixed our criteria, we sell short at 45, the price at the end of September, and proceed again to track the price action of Zombex, detailed in Figure 12-1. After a brief rise in October, the price takes a satisfying dip, then rebounds partway. November ends with a slight rise, but December shows another satisfying drop.

However, in January (along with the stock market in general) Zombex takes a dismaying leap, ending the month at 45½, one-half point higher than where we took our short position.

Note that we use the terms *satisfying* and *dismaying*—for emotional response can never be entirely separated from investment. The aim of the risk and opportunity approach, however, is to temper both euphoria and panic in order to make sure that reason prevails in investment decision-making. That end, you must agree, is as noble as it is rare.

Our resistance to panic is tested anew early in February, when the stock rises to 48, a full point above our predicted high. This development is rather alarming, because we wanted the price to decline in orderly fashion from 45 to somewhere near the predicted low of 33. Instead, the accursed stock is behaving like—well, a stock!

At 48, our short position shows a paper loss of $3 a share. Should we cover here and take the loss? Most people would probably do just that, because the panic associated with a $3 loss on a

Figure 12-1: More tracking

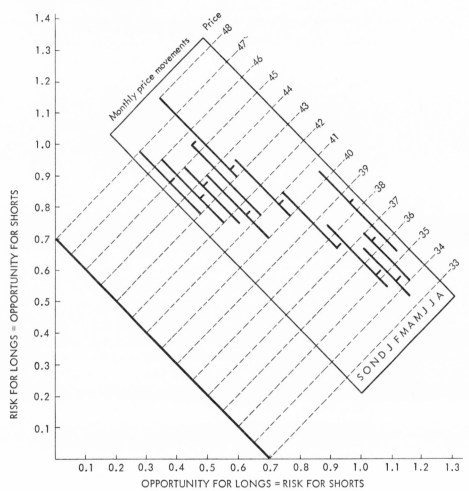

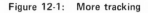

short position is many times greater than that
associated with a $3 loss on a long position—even
though the same amount of money is involved.

It is true that whenever the predicted high or
low is breached, a reassessment of the fundamen-

tal assumptions is in order. Actually, if the assessment is performed on a continuous basis, as it should be, a small breach will come as no surprise. In the case of Zombex, just to be sure, we check the basics once more, decide against panic, and hold our short position, confident that the stock's volatility move on the downside is overdue.

Our faith in our figures is rewarded when the price plunges. We cover in May at 37, with risk 0.2, opportunity 0.5. In June the price drops to 33½, but by then we are free and clear, with a gain of 18 percent in eight months.

In this example, as in the previous one, no use of debt leverage has been considered. But with 50 percent margin, for example, profits would be double those shown (less costs). Profits on the short sale would be decreased by the amount of any dividend paid by Zombex during the time the short position was held.

In our short-selling example we assumed a longer time period for achieving our ends than was assumed in our long-buying example. Thus, the annualized returns in the two cases are not comparable, and could easily have been reversed in magnitude by the whims of the marketplace.

Note that all of the price "tracking" described in this and the preceding chapter takes place within the volatility trap (with one slight breach to illustrate human error). The breakdown into more limited price fluctuations occurring within the larger volatility trap helped, we hope, to illustrate some of the problems that can arise, and how they can be handled.

Chapter 13

Forecasting highs and lows

CHAPTER 13. FORECASTING
HIGHS AND LOWS

RANDOM WALK AND THE
GREATER FOOL THEORY

Most investors, amateur and professional alike, have no real idea which way the price of a stock will go in the future. They may hope, or pray a lot, or invoke occult powers of various kinds—but they do not *know*. In fact, there is a theory— quite popular now—that says it is impossible to forecast stock prices. This is known as the "Random Walk theory."

One of the fascinating parts of the general theory holds, however, that the greater the risk taken, the greater, on average, the reward. A similar idea, long known to less academic inves- tors, is called the "Greater Fool theory."

Strange to say, the dependence of many money managers on the Greater Fool theory is real, and there is even a degree of security for them in practicing it. Rather late in every bull market comes a scramble for the most popular stocks— usually the very ones that languished at low prices for months or years before the scramble began. That is to say, most of the profit potential has been used up before the buying fever hits. Nevertheless, the concerted buying is self- fulfilling, since it confirms the wisdom of the money managers as demand pushes prices higher and higher.

But finally the closeout phase of the Greater Fool theory must be activated if paper profits are to be made concrete; those who have bought at high prices must now find a greater fool on whom

to unload at still higher prices. Some lucky
unloaders, the only moderately greedy, get out in
time, but a sudden scarcity of greater fools
develops. All the big institutional investors—
hampered by the illiquidity of their vast assets—
take their lumps (along with minor league fools)
as stock prices plummet.

Nevertheless, because almost all of them have
concentrated on the same group of stocks ("nifty
fifty," "vestal virgins," or whatever), the money
managers are secure in the knowledge that they
have passed the acid test of "prudence" in their
handling of other people's assets. Who can
criticize them for investing in the same sinkers as
other prudent money managers? The whole
process has come to be known as "the Performance Game." Incidentally, this game provides
much of the statistical basis on which theorists
have concluded that no one can beat the averages.

A SYSTEM BASED ON LOGIC

The risk and opportunity approach that we
advocate is different from the one pictured
(perhaps with a bit of hyperbole) above; in fact,
it is different from any other we have heard
about—and we have done some research.

For one thing, our approach limits buying to
times when opportunity is measurably high and
risk is low, so that a large—but relatively low-
risk—profit potential can be realized. In contrast
to the conventional—and academically backed—
wisdom that high risks must be taken to achieve
high rewards, our approach shows that for a given
level of price volatility, the lower the risk the
greater the opportunity for gain. Moreover, if the

price is right, a stock of high volatility can be less risky, as well as much more profitable, than one of low volatility.

By setting rigorous criteria for buying and modest criteria for selling after a price rise, we capture the bulk of the profit potential, and leave the remainder to those who choose to fight over the question of who is the greatest fool. This fact is brought out most vividly by comparison of our portfolio control models; we have one for practitioners of the Greater Fool theory, too (see Chapter 20).

PREDICTING HIGHS AND LOWS
FROM EARNINGS ESTIMATES

The estimation of future high and low prices is, of course, a key part of our system, and the subject deserves at least one entire volume of its own. Our book *Risk and Opportunity* is not devoted entirely to forecasting highs and lows, but it does illustrate a number of approaches.

One of the methods detailed in the book makes use of estimated earnings, and projects recent high-earnings and low-earnings ratios to predict highs and lows for the period immediately following.

An outstanding example of how this method can work was presented by du Pont. Using Value Line's estimates of earnings per share for the current year and for the year following, $7.10 and $7.90, respectively, we forecast the future high and low by multiplying the current year's (just ending) high, 158.0, and low, 129.5, by the factor 7.90/7.10. The results were a predicted high of 175.8 for the following year, and a predicted low of 144.1. The actual high and low, both realized during the first quarter of the new year, were 175.5 and 144.3—only fractions of a point from the predictions.

This example represents an unusually good adjustment of prices to expected earnings, even though Value Line's estimates, as the final reports showed, were somewhat off the mark. It is not unusual, as in the case of du Pont, for price range forecasts for the coming year to be realized in whole or in part (that is, either high or low, or both) within the first quarter. This fact points up the need for constant tracking and revision as new information becomes available.

When the yearly earnings were finally in, du Pont reported $7.33 and $8.50, respectively, for the two years covered in the study. Had the final figures been estimated accurately earlier, the yearly high of 184.4 could have been approximated as follows: $8.50/7.33 \times 158.0 = 183.2$—an error of well under 1 percent.

However, such accuracy is *not* necessary in order to apply the risk and opportunity approach with outstanding success. In the book *Risk and Opportunity,* the method of forecasting highs and lows just demonstrated for du Pont was applied to the other stocks included in the 30 Dow Jones Industrials. Some predictions (all were based on Value Line's estimates, which were understandably subject to error) were off the mark or were not fulfilled completely during the first quarter. Nevertheless, the overall results were quite remarkable.

Rating the 30 stocks solely on the basis of opportunity, a portfolio of the top six was selected. At the end of the first quarter, the six showed an average gain of 12.6 percent (over 50 percent annualized) compared to a 4.3 percent rise for all of the 30 stocks in the Dow. Even more striking, the 24 stocks rejected for having too little opportunity gained on average only 2.2 percent during the quarter.

Our rather simple screen spotted three of the six stocks which showed the greatest price appreciation, and the other three selected were well above average in performance. The six stocks which actually performed best made an average gain of 18.0 percent, compared with the 12.6 percent of the portfolio we selected. In other words, our simple method of selection, based solely on rankings for opportunity, produced 70 percent of the gain available to an investor with perfect predictive powers.

There is no doubt that even better results could have been obtained with less stringent constraints and a broader field of selection than were offered by the rather dull Dow Jones Industrials. This fact is illustrated in our book by a study applying the same forecasting method to 10 institutional favorites, and ranking the top two for opportunity during the first quarter. Although the 10 included such Dow Jones Industrials as Sears, General Electric, and Westinghouse, the stocks with the greatest appreciation potential were obviously Polaroid and R. J. Reynolds, which were in the very highest opportunity area of the R/O diagram. These quickly advanced 43 percent and 29 percent, respectively.

At their highs, which were almost exactly those predicted, both Polaroid and Reynolds showed zero opportunity and maximum risk. They were then beautiful candidates for short selling. As it developed, both suffered truly massive losses in subsequent periods.

(The recurring references made in this chapter and in others to our earlier book, *Risk and Opportunity: A New Approach to Stock Market Profits,* may lead some suspicious reader to feel that we are recommending its purchase. Suspicious Reader will be right.)

Chapter 14

Swinging with the market

CHAPTER 14. SWINGING
WITH THE MARKET

In the previous chapter we illustrated how earnings, and even earnings estimates (which are often inaccurate), affect the prices of stocks. Over the long term, real earnings—rather than those dreamed up by company management and certified by complaisant accountants—are the most important determinants of stock prices.

This is as it should be, for, both theoretically and practically, the current price of any company's stock should reflect the present value of the company's stream of future earnings—which accrue to stockholders in the form of dividends, or are reinvested in the company to increase the stock's value per share.

Naturally, investor *expectations* as to dividends, growth potentials, management capabilities, and how the company will fare in the general economy play a large part in determining the price/earnings ratios for individual companies.

After earnings—and often independent of them—the most important determinant of stock price swings is the fluctuation of the overall market itself. This is commonly measured by such indexes as the Dow Jones Industrials, Standard & Poor's 500, or the New York Stock Exchange (NYSE) Composite, which includes all the stocks listed on the Big Board.

There are countless reasons for bull and bear markets—ranging from the state of the economy to the madness of crowds. Regardless of their logic or lack of logic, markets have great power to sweep along with them all stocks—good, bad, and indifferent. This power must be reckoned with and, if possible, utilized.

Obviously, the depths of bear markets, when risk is low and opportunity high, are great times to buy. However, it is at these very times that the psychological atmosphere, heavy with pessimism, is so rampant that buying is inhibited (and short selling of the most dangerous kind picks up).

At the other end of the swing, near bull market peaks, when risk is high and opportunity hovers near zero, euphoric crowd psychology induces buying fervor at record volume.

The approach using risk and opportunity, which quantifies these important qualities, is specifically designed to eliminate errors due to such emotional responses, so that the investor can make logical decisions under stress.

Although a few stocks sometimes buck the sweeping trends of bull and bear markets, most stocks do respond in greater or lesser degree to market swings—often even on a daily basis. Thus, if the market is up (or down) for the day, month, or year, we expect our American Telephone, or whatever, to move in the same direction.

Comovement of a stock's price with changes in the level of the overall market, represented by one index or another, can be a useful tool in making investment decisions. As we've mentioned, the beta coefficient—beta, for short—is a measure of a stock's comovement with the market. In its simplest and most useful form, beta indicates how much the price of a stock will move in response to a given move in the overall market. For example, a beta of 1.5 for Chrysler means that a 10 percent move in the NYSE Composite (if that is the index used as the base) will be reflected by a 15 percent move in Chrysler's price and in the same direction.

Of course, the correlation is not perfect: There are leads and lags. But on average we can predict with a fair degree of accuracy that the relationships will hold well enough to permit forecasts of future highs and lows—the bases for measuring risk and opportunity.

Price volatility, as we have seen, can be measured by range variability. In our familiar symbols, $V = (H - L)/A$. Now, if we designate the volatility of a stock by the symbol V_s and that of the market over the same period of time by V_m, beta is simply V_s/V_m. The beta just described is the Poor Boy beta introduced in Chapter 3.

Many variations of beta are available from various sources; their utility varies with their method of computation. Some beta researchers trace price action back for decades in an effort to get a number that will hold still for them. However, the Poor Boy beta makes the simple assumption that price volatility during the immediate past will continue in approximately the same degree into the immediate future. (For stocks which fluctuate widely from year to year, using an average beta for the past three or five years might be wise, but there seems little justification for delving further into history than that.)

In a study detailed in the book *Risk and Opportunity*, Poor Boy betas for a year just finished were used to estimate price behavior in the next quarter. For this study, the market base used was the Dow Jones Industrial Index, which showed a maximum rise of 6.7 percent during the quarter. The magnitude of this rise could have been approximated in the same manner in which prices are forecast for individual stocks; for example, on the basis of earnings estimates for the Dow index (which appear from time to time in various financial publications).

The individual stocks of the Dow 30 were used in the study. For each stock, the high for the quarter was determined by multiplying its beta by the change in the Dow index times the starting price, then adding the result to the starting price. On average, the betas of the individual stocks making up the Dow were 2.12, compared to 1.00 for the index itself.

As for the results, the predicted highs missed the actual highs by an average 3.1 points, above or below (about 4.5 percent), but the average *net* difference of the predicted highs from the actual highs was only +0.5 point (0.7 percent).

Even more effective than pinpointing actual prices is selecting stocks on the basis of their *rankings* for price appreciation. Stated another way, it is even more useful to spot the top performers than to forecast their exact highs.

To illustrate: If the investment strategy had been to select the top five stocks, the simple screening method just described would have gained an average 20 percent during the first quarter, compared to 25 percent for the actual top five and a rise of 11 percent for the average Dow 30 stock. Had the choice been narrowed to four stocks, the method would have scored 23 percent during the quarter, compared to a theoretical gain of 26 percent for an investor with an infallible crystal ball.

The study just summarized demonstrates how price comovement with the market (or swinging with the market, if you prefer) can be used to forecast highs, one of the important variables in the measurement of risk and opportunity. Lows can be forecast in similar fashion to obtain the other unknown variable.

The method is admittedly simplistic, so, like any other system yet devised or any that will be conjured up in the future, it will not be effective for every stock in every situation (otherwise it would self-destruct). It should therefore be used along with the various alternative approaches discussed in *Risk and Opportunity* in order to give proper weight to other important factors that influence stock prices.

Price comovement with the market is, of course, just as important in selling short as it is in buying long.

Chapter 15

The effect of errors in forecasting

CHAPTER 15. THE EFFECT
OF ERRORS IN FORECASTING

Toward the end of Chapter 10, which explained the use of the volatility trap in making buy and sell decisions, we gave a partial answer to the question, What can go wrong? This chapter expands on that answer, and weighs the consequences of errors.

Since the unknown variables needed to calculate the risk and opportunity of any stock are its future high and low, it is obvious that errors in forecasting these prices may lead to errors in timing decisions, and thus affect the efficiency of the system itself.

However, even though highs and lows cannot be predicted with unerring accuracy, they need only be approximated for the system to be highly effective. This was demonstrated rather dramatically in Chapters 13 and 14, which described how simple screens applied to a group of actual stocks were used to forecast the winners. In the examples cited, small errors did not prevent the selection process from being highly efficient, if somewhat less than perfect.

The effect of errors in forecasting can also be illustrated by hypothetical numerical examples. Let's assume that we are considering a highly volatile stock whose future high and low we estimate to be 30 and 10, respectively. Volatility is therefore $(30 - 10)/20 = 1.00$.

Because of this high volatility, which can kill us as well as help us, we decide to play it very close to the chest, not buying until the price drops to the point where risk will be only 0.1, at

which point opportunity will be 1.9, for a safe
O/R ratio of 19 to 1.

At risk equals 0.1, price will be 11—only $1
above the forecast low, as our formula tells us:
$P = L + .25(H + L)R = 10 + .25(30 + 10)0.1 = 11.$

Now, let's consider the effect of 10 percent
errors in forecasting the high or the low, or both,
and all possible combinations of those errors.

Table 15-1 details all possible results of 10
percent errors in forecasting, and Figure 15-1
shows how the volatility lines shift under the
various assumptions. (Table and figure are corre-
lated by "case" letters a to i.)

As the table shows, the high—originally forecast
at 30—can be as high as 33 or as low as 27, and
the low—forecast at 10—can be as high as 11 or
as low as 9. Because, on the basis of our original
forecasts, we have decided to buy at 11 or below,
there will be no failure to make a purchase in any
of the cases shown, in spite of the forecasting
errors.

Although we have set very strict criteria (risk
0.1 and opportunity 1.9) for this very volatile
stock, prudence dictates that we be much less
demanding when setting sell criteria (another way
of saying "Take the money and run"). Therefore,
we decide to sell when risk, on our original
assumptions as to high and low, rises to 1.6, at
which point opportunity will have dropped to
0.4. There's plenty of gain potential left, but let's
leave some crumbs for the greater fools to fight
over.

When risk is 1.6, the price of the stock will
be 26. The table shows that, in spite of errors in
the forecast high, we would sell out with room
to spare in every case. Our profit, in case you are

Table 15-1: Effect of 10 percent errors in forecasting highs and lows

Case	High	Low	Avg.	H-L	V	Buy at 11			Sell at 26		
						C^*	R	O	C^*	R	O
Original forecast . . . . a	30	10	20.0	20	1.00	−0.90	0.10	1.90	+0.60	1.60	0.40
High, low 10% high . . . . b	33	11	22.0	22	1.00	−1.00	0.00	2.00	+0.36	1.36	0.64
High, low 10% low c	27	9	18.0	18	1.00	−0.78	0.22	1.78	+0.89	1.89	0.11
High 10% high, low 10% low . . . . . . d	33	9	21.0	24	1.14	−0.95	0.19	2.09	+0.48	1.62	0.66
High 10% low, low 10% high . . . e	27	11	19.0	16	0.84	−0.84	0.00	1.68	+0.74	1.58	0.10
High 10% high, low on target . . . . . f	33	10	21.5	23	1.07	−0.98	0.09	2.05	+0.42	1.49	0.65
High 10% low, low on target . . . . . g	27	10	18.5	17	0.92	−0.81	0.11	1.73	+0.81	1.73	0.11
High on target, low 10% high . . . . h	30	11	20.5	19	0.93	−0.93	0.00	1.86	+0.54	1.47	0.39
High on target, low 10% low i	30	9	19.5	21	1.08	−0.87	0.21	1.95	+0.67	1.75	0.41

*The algebraic signs for C, the current price factor, are for risk; the signs are reversed in calculating opportunity.

interested in such mundane matters, would be 136 percent on the $11 per share investment— even without using margin.

It is instructive to examine Table 15-1 to see how risk and opportunity values varied under the various assumptions. We assumed that risk would be 0.1, but due to various errors in forecasting, it actually ranged from zero to 0.22. Opportunity, which we assumed to be 1.90, actually ranged from 1.68 to 2.09.

At the other end of the transaction, selling at 26, we assumed that risk would be 1.6 and opportunity 0.4. Due to forecasting errors, risk at the time of sale could have been as low as 1.36 or as high as 1.89, while opportunity could have ranged from 0.10 to 0.66.

The table also shows that volatility, with a value of 1.00 under the original assumptions, might have varied between 0.84 and 1.14 because of errors in forecasting. Consequently, the volatility lines, as seen in Figure 15-1, show a spread from Case *e*, the least volatile, outward to Case *d*, the most volatile. Case *b*, with forecasts 10 percent high, and Case *c*, 10 percent low, have the same 1.00 volatility as the original forecast, so they share the same volatility line. However, their buying and selling points are different, to reflect the different degrees of risk and opportunity at the time of purchase and sale.

The main lesson to be learned from the above exercise is that one need not be a perfect fore- caster for the system to work effectively. This is fortunate, because there is no such thing as a perfect forecaster.

Although we *estimate* future highs and lows— such estimates are essential for calculating risk

Figure 15-1:   Effect of 10 percent errors in forecasting highs and lows

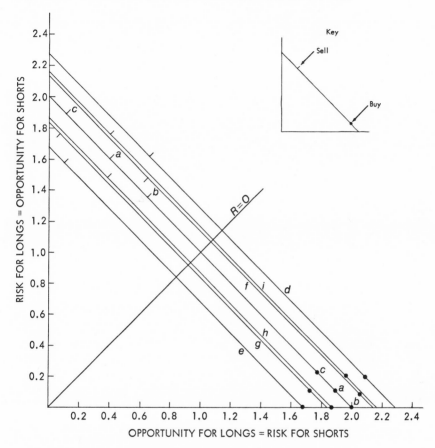

Note: Lowercase letters refer to the "cases" in Table 15-1.

and opportunity—we're not conceited enough to believe we're going to pinpoint them. Our method, while taking advantage of the wide fluctuations between highs and lows, operates in the secure and fertile area well inside them.

Chapter 16

Dream along with Dow Jones

CHAPTER 16. DREAM
ALONG WITH DOW JONES

Having dwelt on human fallibility, perhaps to excess, in the previous chapter, let us now unwind by imagining how we might have prospered had we been able to forecast accurately the price action of the 30 Dow Jones Industrials at the start of a recent year.

We have made the assumption that at the start of the year, with current prices then known, we were able to forecast accurately the highs and lows for each stock that actually occurred during the year. From these data we calculated volatility, risk, and opportunity for the full year. Then, using current prices at the end of the second, third, and fourth quarters, we determined the values of risk and opportunity on those dates.

We'll spare you all the tedious calculations; the results are summarized on three R/O diagrams, Figures 16-1A, 16-1B, and 16-1C. Ten members of the Dow Jones family are plotted on each figure, and which stock appears on which figure was determined solely by the desire to minimize crowding of the volatility lines. Each line is labeled with the name of the stock it represents.

The risk and opportunity values at the start of the year are indicated by zeros opposite each plotted dot, as shown by the key on each diagram. Also indicated are the risk and opportunity values as they stood at midyear (2), at the end of the third quarter (3), and at year-end (4). Values at highs and lows, of course, occur at the extremes of the volatility lines.

We do not intend a guided tour of these O/R

Figure 16-1A: Risk and opportunity ranges for Dow Jones Industrials

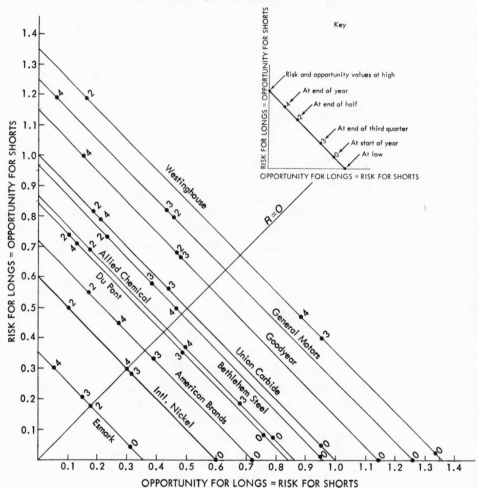

117

Figure 16-1B: Risk and opportunity ranges for Dow Jones Industrials

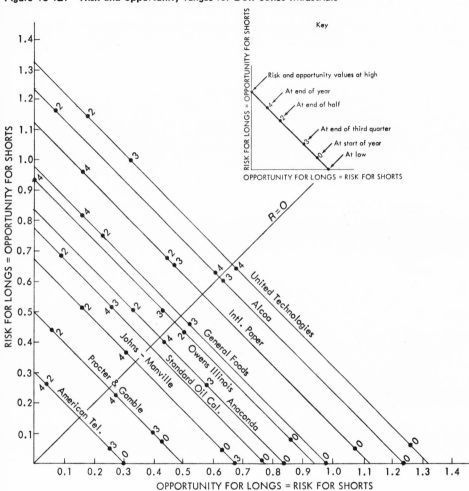

118

Figure 16-1C: Risk and opportunity ranges for Dow Jones Industrials

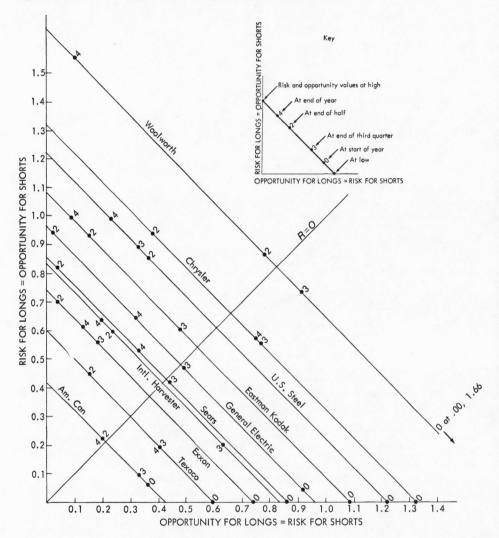

diagrams, detailing the fortunes of each stock throughout the year. Some stocks rose in quite regular pattern. Many jumped ahead during the first half, then subsided. Others seemed determined to show how cyclical they could be. All obeyed Morgan's Law, demonstrating the profit potential in price fluctuations.

The reader can dream his or her own dreams, secure in the knowledge that every single stock was caught in its own narrow volatility trap. What striking feats of investment prowess were possible for anyone who could set those traps in advance! (As we have seen, the traps can be approximated, which would indicate that a reasonable facsimile of Dreamland is also available.)

You, the reader, might find it worthwhile to study these O/R diagrams, and ask yourself the questions: With these volatility traps in hand at the start of the year (but not knowing the situation in later quarters), which stocks would you have rated top buys? At what point, if any, would you have sold them? Can you spot any good short sales?

Now ask yourself the same questions, knowing the situation at the end of: (a) the second quarter, (b) the third quarter, and (c) the year.

You are not expected to know all the answers yet, by any means, but you should know enough by this time to make some educated guesses. Besides, the exercise will serve to increase your appreciation of the control models when you get to them in Chapter 20. Then, you might well return to the three illustrations of this chapter with a tracing of one or more of the control models to place over the O/R diagrams. You just might be astonished at how effective the controls can be.

Chapter 17

The uses of
short selling

CHAPTER 17. THE USES
OF SHORT SELLING

The principal use of short selling, as this book should make clear, is to take profitable and methodical advantage of the downside phases of stock price fluctuations. How to coordinate selling short with buying long, and how to manage a portfolio most efficiently by using control models, are the subjects of the three following, and final, chapters.

Stated briefly, the aim of this book is to show how to make maximum use of capital for any degree of risk selected by the investor, and to accomplish this by taking advantage of price fluctuations through the use of risk and opportunity measurement to guide both buying long and selling short.

Short selling itself has other uses which are already well known, so we won't give much space to them here. If you are a neophyte investor, we refer you for details to your broker or to some standard printed work, such as the *Stock Market Handbook,* edited by Frank G. Zarb and Gabriel T. Kerekes (Homewood, Ill.: Dow Jones-Irwin, 1970). And if you are a professional, you already know all the answers.

We offer here only some brief comments on selling short (1) against the box, (2) for arbitrage, (3) for hedging, and (4) for merger arbitrage.

SELLING SHORT AGAINST THE BOX

This type of short sale is ordinarily used to carry over profits from one tax year to the next—

when, it is hoped, tax treatment on the gain may be more favorable. Perhaps a general tax cut is coming up, or you expect to be in a lower tax bracket. Or perhaps you expect the price of the stock to drop, and you want to protect your gain. In any case, the stock is already owned by the short seller—that is, it's in the "box"—at the time the seller shorts an equal number of shares. No tax on the gain is due until the following year, when the short sale is covered by the delivery of the stock from the box, thereby closing out both the long and the short position.

SELLING SHORT FOR ARBITRAGE

When securities (or anything else) are selling for one price in one market (say, New York) and for a different price in another market (say, London), a profit can possibly be made by simultaneously buying at the lower price and selling short at the higher price.

In the case of the ordinary investor, the profit possibilities are largely theoretical, if not chimerical. For one thing, the costs involved (commissions and so on) are usually more than enough to wipe out any price differential. Also, there are mechanical difficulties in buying and selling "simultaneously" at markets in different locations.

Arbitrage can be profitable (and virtually riskless) for the professional insider who can skip commissions and use an efficient communications system which is already a part of the operation.

For what it's worth, the uptick rule does not apply to this type of "technical short sale." The sale is entered as a "short-exempt" sale, and can be made at any time, regardless of previous price action.

ARBITRAGE WITH CONVERTIBLE SECURITIES

Another kind of arbitrage using a technical short sale—and one which offers a bit more opportunity for the ordinary investor—is possible when there is a disparity in price between one security of a company and another security of the same company into which the first is convertible. Securities convertible into common stock include convertible preferred stock, convertible bonds, warrants, and put and call options. Here again, the profit is quick and virtually riskless, but success depends on catching someone asleep at the switch.

HEDGING

When long and short positions in the stock and convertible of the same company are held in a portfolio, rather than turned over quickly in an arbitrage operation, a true hedge is in operation.

The type of "hedging" which so-called hedge funds use is not true hedging, because these funds take long positions in some companies and short positions in other companies. If the longs go down and the shorts go up, the supposed hedge is blown to smithereens. (More on "hedge funds" in the following chapter.)

In contrast, there is little or no risk in the true hedge, where a price move in one security is generally compensated for by a price move in another security related to it. Convertibles ordinarily sell at a premium over the common stock into which they are convertible, but it is not unusual to find a convertible bond, say, selling at or near par with the common stock—and patient investors wait for such favorable conditions to come along.

Under such conditions, an investor might well go long the bonds and short the stock. If the price of the stock rises (meaning a loss on the short position), the price of the bond will go up at least enough to compensate, and interest on the bond will normally more than cover any dividends that might be payable on the stock. Should the price of the stock go down (resulting in a gain on the short position), the bond price will probably decline proportionately less, because of its higher investment quality and yield. In either case, appreciable disparities in prices can be taken advantage of by closing out both positions and pocketing the difference—if, indeed, any remains after transaction costs.

Professional advisory services offer assistance in assessing the investment worth of convertible securities selling above par, as most do. Warrants, for example, always sell at a premium, even when their convertible value is zilch. Readers interested in this subject will have no trouble finding enticing ads in the financial press.

Our own general objection to true hedging is that, in effect, it is playing the left hand against the right. As prices change, money goes from one pocket to another, but the net change seldom justifies the amount of money tied up in the long position (although no additional deposit is required to carry the short). Therefore, the true hedge seems to be an inefficient use of capital—a

low-opportunity trade-off for an undeniably low
risk. Why not choose high opportunity along with
low risk?

ARBITRAGING POTENTIAL MERGERS

Mergers and takeover activities reached a cres-
cendo during the "funny-money" bull market of
the 1960s. These activities, although seemingly
more subdued now, are still going strong. Arbitrage possibilities occur frequently in merger
situations.

Mergers can be friendly or unfriendly; in the
stockholders' interests or against them. In the
simplest case, everyone concerned—officers,
directors, and stockholders of both companies—
agrees that a merger would be beneficial. *Synergy,*
often described as two plus two equals five, was
the corporate buzzword of the 60s; it meant that
the whole was greater than the sum of its parts.
The word has fallen into disrepute, quite possibly
because experience indicated that the equation
was more often on the order of two plus two
equals three. (Some of the parts, it seemed, were
going down the hole.) Thus, a backwash of
divestitures followed the urge to merge.

Given agreement that a merger would benefit
both companies, and agreement also that the
shares of both companies have been fairly priced
by the market, the corporate marriage could be
consummated by a simple exchange of shares of
the principal company for those of the company
absorbed. In such idyllic cases, there is little
opportunity for arbitrage.

In the more usual merger, even if it is friendly,
the officers and shareholders of the company

being gobbled up insist on a sweetener—a premium for their shares over a dollar-for-dollar exchange on the basis of market value. In such a situation, an arbitrageur might take advantage of the disparity in prices by selling short shares of the acquiring company and going long an equivalent number of shares of the company being absorbed.

However, merger arbitrage, unlike the true article, is fraught with risk, because of the real, but unquantifiable, uncertainty that the deal will be consummated. When merger plans fall through, the shorts go up and the longs go down.

The prudent, and probably the more profitable, course of investment action would seem to lie in situations where both risk and opportunity *can* be measured.

Chapter 18

The opportunity fund: A better hedge fund

CHAPTER 18. THE OPPORTUNITY FUND: A BETTER HEDGE FUND

During the bull market of the 60s, certain daring, predominantly young, stock market gunslingers were so successful at the performance game that they were immortalized in a glossy, outsized picture book entitled *The New Breed on Wall Street.* (It was published, sad to relate, at about the same time that the "Soaring Sixties" were souring for most of them.)

Many of this so-called New Breed—those right at the top of the heap—were riding to riches and glory on a then rather newfangled financial vehicle called the "hedge fund."

Like many names that catch on quickly with the public, this was a misnomer. The hedge fund did not employ true hedging; that is, taking a short position in a company security that is convertible into another security of the same company in which a long position is held. A true hedge, for example, would be a long position in a company's convertible bond balanced by a short position of exactly the number of common shares into which the bond is convertible.

In our book on hedge funds, *Hedgemanship,* we define them as: private or public pools of investment capital that seek to minimize risk by "hedging" their long positions in some stocks by taking short positions in other stocks, and that usually pursue their goal of maximum capital appreciation by employing leverage to maximize performance.

Properly used, the hedge fund is a truly superior investment device. By selling short and buying long, it can prosper in both bear and bull markets; and if it does these things well, its success can be multiplied by debt leverage as well as the leverage made possible by the use of warrants, puts and calls, and other forms of options.

During their days of glory the hedge funds *seemed* to be performing miracles because they were riding the highfliers in a wild bull market, while abandoning short selling and using leverage to the hilt. When the market topped out and started downward in late 1968, the funds got caught with their shorts not merely down, but completely missing. Their highfliers could fly in only one direction now—down—and, being very volatile, they plunged even faster than the market. To make matters worse, their leverage was then working against them, leveraging their losses.

Hedge fund managers, who couldn't bring themselves to believe that the fiesta was over, were slow to move out of longs and into shorts— and when they did so they chose the wrong stocks to short, those which were perverse enough to rally, or at least refuse to subside without a struggle. Finally, many of the distraught managers—in what was really a confession that they didn't know *what* to do—abandoned the two pillars of successful hedge fund operation, short selling and leverage.

The whole disaster is described in gory detail in *Hedgemanship.* The main aim of the book, however, was not merely to document what the hedge funds had done wrong, but to provide guidelines and methods for their successful operation.

Risk and opportunity measurement, in fact, had its beginning in *Hedgemanship,* in what we dubbed the "riskop factor." This was used as a means of weighting the amount of a fund's assets that should be invested in its long and short positions at any given time.

The book also described a method, based on moving averages of stock market advances and declines, for keeping the hedge fund in step with the overall market. This was a useful device, because one supposed advantage of the hedge fund is that its manager can take a *pragmatic* approach to investment. As the book put the matter: The hedge fund manager "need not make elaborate forecasts based on such factors as economic conditions, the trend of interest rates, money supply, inflation, war, peace, sunspots, or how he's getting along with his wife. He can simply adjust the proportion of his longs and shorts to keep in tune with market conditions as they are revealed to him by the market itself."

The method of keeping in step with the market by using ratios of moving averages of advances and declines was illustrated in some detail in our *Barron's* article of October 4, 1971, "Hedging Does Work: The Technique Is Better than Some Who Claim to Use It" (a title fortuitously conceived by the editor).

In *Risk and Opportunity,* we describe how the long/short ratios determined by the advance/decline moving averages can be weighted by opportunity measures. To illustrate briefly: Suppose that at the moment the four-week moving average of the advances stands at 1100, while that for the declines is 400. This would indicate, before weighting for opportunity, that the current value of longs in the portfolio should be about 1100/1500, or 73 percent, and that the balance of 27 percent should be invested in the shorts.

Now the value of weighting for opportunity becomes evident. The 73/27 ratio of our example indicates (as we have learned from experience) that the market is nearing a peak. Weighting continuously for opportunity allows the manager to take profits in longs as the market booms, while shifting assets into shorts in preparation for the inevitable downturn. This is how it operates: As prices get near their peaks, opportunity values drop in the longs and rise in the shorts. At the moment we are considering, the shorts in our portfolio might average about 0.9 in opportunity, while opportunity for the longs might have dropped to about 0.1. The weighted long/short ratio, then, should be approximately $(73 \times 0.1)/(27 \times 0.9)$, meaning that 23 percent of the total assets should be in long positions and 77 percent in shorts.

Near bear market bottoms the situation would be reversed. Profits on the shorts would be taken on the way down as their opportunity values waned, and the money would move increasingly into longs as their prices dropped and they came to meet suitable opportunity criteria.

No matter what the position of the overall market, the individual stocks in the portfolio would have to satisfy the risk and opportunity standards set for them, and the allocation of funds between longs and shorts would always be based on market trend, weighted for opportunity.

Low-risk, high-yield securities, such as Treasury bills, can be very useful near market extremes. Near market tops, their opportunity values (as calculated by the formula given in Chapter 5) may well exceed the opportunity in long positions in any available stocks, so funds not invested on the short side can be put into money market instruments instead. Likewise, near bear market bottoms funds not invested long in stocks can be put into money market items instead of short positions in stocks. There is really no point in having funds invested in positions, either long or short, if the numbers tell us that risk is excessive and opportunity is pushing zero.

We call a fund managed under the principles described above an "Opportunity Fund"—and we wouldn't mind at all if investors came to disassociate it forever from the ill-famed hedge funds of the past (whose ill fame, to be fair, was not due to any inherent faults of the funds, but to the faults of their managers).

Chapter 19

Efficient portfolio management

CHAPTER 19. EFFICIENT
PORTFOLIO MANAGEMENT

An *efficient portfolio,* by our definition, is one which maintains maximum opportunity for a given level of risk, or which maintains minimum risk for a given level of opportunity.

This definition applies both to buying long and selling short. Because stocks go down in price just as readily as they go up, profit can be realized from either movement. It seems to us that any portfolio management system that aims to maximize profits, but ignores the profit potential in short selling, is negligent. It's rather like being in a footrace and using only one foot.

Nearly all professional money managers, the big institutions in particular, are prohibited from using short selling, so they avoid it as they would avoid driving the wrong way on a one-way street. Therefore, in down markets the only defensive measure available to them is to liquidate part of their holdings in common stock, and put the money into such "near-cash" money market instruments as Treasury bills and commercial paper.

However, because of their size, the big institutions—banks, insurance companies, mutual funds, foundations, pension funds—can liquidate on only a very limited scale. For most of them, 10 or 15 percent is considered a large cash position. It helps, but the 85 or 90 percent remaining in stocks is taking a beating along with the general market.

Because of the constraints on their options—illiquidity and the inability to sell short—the big institutions must be particularly careful to maintain the maximum portfolio efficiency that the constraints will allow. Portfolio management based on the use of risk and opportunity measurement is therefore even more important to institutions than it is to individual investors who are not subject to the constraints. Putting the matter another way, individual investors should be able to perform much better than institutions (which on average have indeed been unable to even equal the performance of the overall market).

What follows is intended for both individual and institutional investors. Those prohibited from selling short do not enjoy all the options of those who can sell short, but the basic steps of portfolio management are the same for both.

Efficient portfolio management can be reduced to six basic steps, all of which are interrelated and constantly interacting:

1. Measurement.
2. Comparison, screening, selection.
3. Timing.
4. Monitoring and control.
5. Maximizing return with minimum risk.
6. Review and adjustment.

These steps, which should be fairly obvious, are discussed in some detail in *Risk and Opportunity*. In the present book, we've tried to minimize rehashing our earlier works, so we'll sketch only the bare essentials here:

Measurement is the basic step on which all the others depend. It is the distillation of all available information into two numbers, the projected high and low, followed by the calculation of risk and opportunity values based on current price; and other measures, such as O/R ratios, based on those values.

Comparison, screening, selection rank all the stocks under consideration according to risk, opportunity, O/R ratio, and related measures (plus special criteria set by each portfolio, such as quality, size, debt ratio, number of shares out, and industry).

Timing is the sum of buy, hold, and sell actions taken to follow whatever criteria are selected for a particular portfolio. (See Chapter 6, "Timing investment decisions.")

Monitoring and control track all the other steps, as well as total portfolio risk and opportunity (which require more conservative criteria than those set for individual stocks) and total portfolio performance (capital gains plus yield).

Maximizing return with minimum risk is the continuous integration of timing, monitoring and control, and review and adjustment.

Review and adjustment is, first, backward-looking—assessing portfolio performance, control criteria, techniques, sources of information, brokers, portfolio managers. Then, in the light of this assessment, forward-looking decisions are made regarding any changes that may be needed.

All of these portfolio management steps are coordinated with the help of control models, which we take up next.

Chapter 20

Control
models

CHAPTER 20. CONTROL MODELS

Portfolio control models are nothing more than our familiar risk/opportunity diagrams upon which are superimposed whatever decision criteria are selected by the portfolio manager. (The diagrams have their computer counterparts, but we won't get involved with those here.)

Figure 20-1 shows a control model in its simplest form. (Let's assume, in this and the next three illustrations, that we're buying long.)

The model says that we will not buy any stock until its price drops to a point where risk is 0.1 or below, and where opportunity is 0.2 or higher. These two numbers therefore delineate the "buy area" (darker shade on the figure).

The model says further that any stock purchased in the buy area will be held only until its price rises to a point where either (a) opportunity drops to 0.2, or (b) risk rises to 0.85. These two figures delineate the "hold area" (light shade), which is indefinite on the right side because no maximum volatility has been specified.

For buying situations in general, it is wise, as well as conservative, to set criteria for buying somewhat tighter than those for selling, in order to make certain of (a) getting in at a good price, and (b) getting out before it is too late—in case our estimates are off the mark. Rationale: If we miss a buy, no harm is done; but if we miss a sell, we could be stuck with a dog for longer than we would like.

Figure 20-2 depicts quite another set of control criteria. These are based on both O/R ratios and volatility limits. This model says: No stock

Figure 20-1: Simple control model

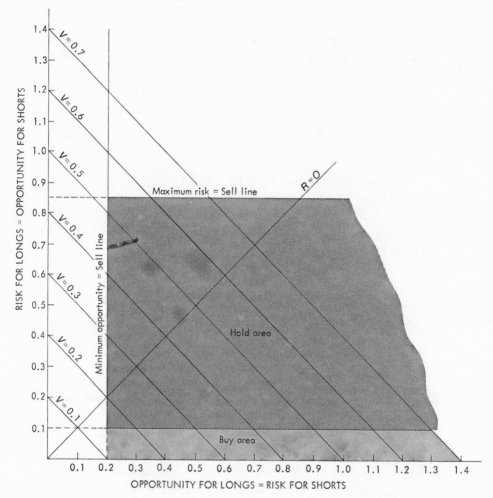

will be bought until its O/R ratio is at least 10 to 1, and no stock will be held beyond the point where its R/O ratio exceeds 2 to 1. Further, no stock will be purchased whose volatility is less than 0.2 (to rule out stocks with too little appre-

Figure 20-2: Control model based on R/O ratio and volatility

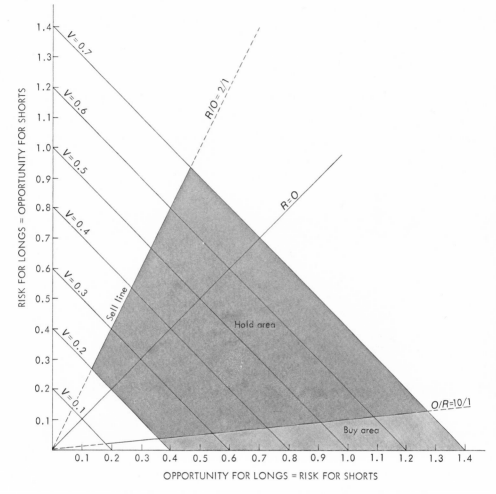

ciation potential) or greater than 0.7 (to put a lid on volatility, because the most volatile stocks are the most difficult to forecast).

Figure 20-3 shows a combination of controlling criteria. This model might well be used by a fairly

Figure 20-3: **Composite control model**

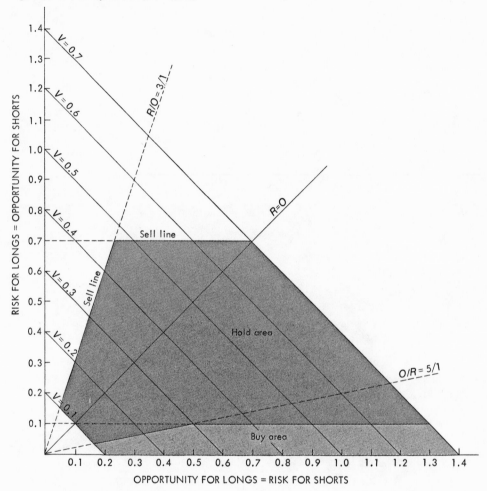

conservative portfolio manager. The model says: Don't buy unless the price is low enough for the *O/R* ratio to be at least 5 to 1, and in no event should risk exceed 0.1. This means, as the diagram makes clear, that the rule "*O/R* at least 5 to 1" applies only if opportunity is under 0.5, and so it allows a higher appreciation potential for stocks of lower volatility. Beyond 0.5 opportunity, the "maximum 0.1 risk" rule takes over, meaning that even higher O/R ratios are demanded.

This model permits purchase of stocks with volatility as low as 0.1 or as high as 0.7, but the risk of holding stocks of higher volatility is limited by the sell line at the 0.7 risk level. A stock with the highest allowable volatility of 0.7 would be sold when the price rose to the point at which risk equaled opportunity. Stocks of lower volatility would be held until risk rose to three times the opportunity value.

The number of possible variations of control models is virtually limitless. The models can accommodate such low-volatility securities as straight bonds and such high-volatility items as stock options and commodity futures. In other words, every investment method or philosophy can be represented on an O/R control model.

There is even a model for those heroic souls who practice the Greater Fool theory—who buy high and expect to sell to some greater fool at a still higher price.

Figure 20-4 is one version of the Greater Fool control model. It says: Buy only stocks that have *proven* to be *real movers*, with a volatility of at least 0.5, and preferably much greater. Buy when the price is already so high that risk has risen to at least 0.90 to 0.95 and opportunity has dropped to 0.05 to 0.10. Then hold until the price reaches its zenith (be very careful to judge this correctly), where risk is at its maximum and opportunity is zero. (Why let go while there's any opportunity left?)

Figure 20-4: **Greater Fool control model**

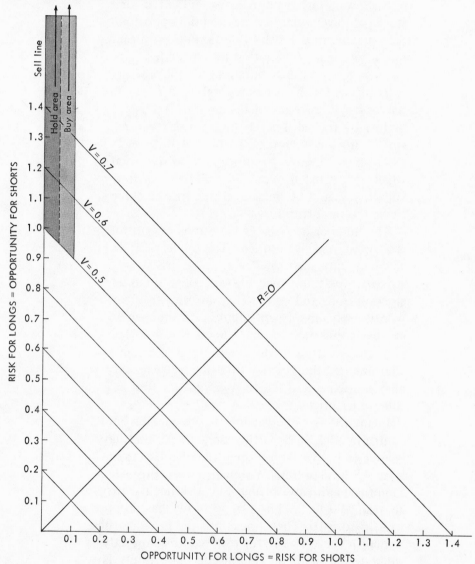

Warning: Due to possible errors in forecasting, the line between the buy and hold areas may be indistinct. In fact, the buy area may even merge into the sell line, forcing the hold area (not precisely as planned) down below and to the right of the buy area. Sorry!

In general, Greater Fool models take over where the sell lines of more conservative models say "Take the money and run."

CONTROL MODELS FOR SELLING SHORT

Like models to control buying long, models to govern short selling are infinite in number, all depending on the wishes and judgment of the investor. And also, as in buying long, the criteria selected to guide selling short should be tighter for taking a position than for closing it out.

Although most short sellers show a strong tendency to close out a short position much sooner than they would a long one with exactly the same risk (and opportunity), there is no reason at all why an investor should not set the identical R and O criteria for selling short that he does for buying long.

Figure 20-5 has done precisely this, setting the same criteria for selling short that Figure 20-3 used for buying long. What this model says is: Don't sell short unless the O/R ratio is at least 5 to 1 and the starting risk is greater than 0.1. Confine short sales to stocks with volatilities between 0.1 and 0.7. Cover short sales when the price drops to the point where risk rises to 0.7 or the R/O ratio rises to 3 to 1, whichever occurs first.

Figure 20-5: Control model for selling short

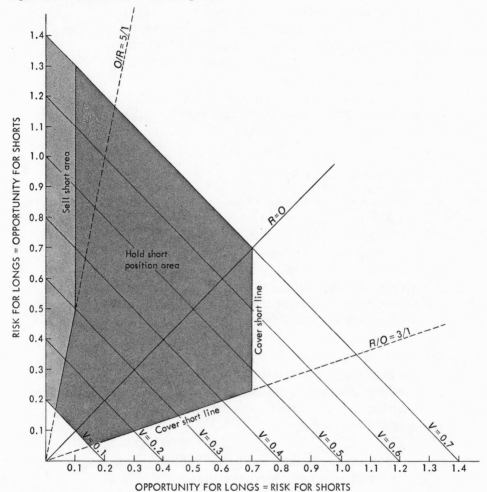

Because the risk and opportunity axes in Figures 20-3 and 20-5 are reversed, one model is a mirror image of the other, rotated 90 degrees.

That's a good way to picture short selling, in fact—as a mirror image of buying long. So (for those of you who have not yet tried it), why not go along with Alice and step through the looking glass. You may discover, as she did, a personal wonderland, and also find that it offers more opportunity than you've found to date on *this* side of the mirror, where it's awfully crowded.

The final three figures demonstrate the utility of control models for both buying long and selling short.

Figure 20-6 shows the control model of Figure 20-2 superimposed on Figure 16-1C, which diagramed the risk and opportunity values of ten of the 30 Dow Jones Industrials. We see that at the start of the year eight of the ten stocks, from volatile Chrysler to more stable Texaco, were priced in the buy area. Only Woolworth exceeded the maximum allowable volatility. The other exception, American Can, initially overpriced, subsequently dropped down into the buy area.

Before the end of the second quarter, price increases had driven the eight best buys completely through the hold area, piercing the sell line and assuring substantial profits while limiting risk. Before year-end, all of the same eight had achieved their highs, and five of these had suffered price retreats sufficient to drop opportunity below risk. Near their highs, all ten stocks were possible candidates for short selling.

Figure 20-7 shows control model 20-3 superimposed on the O/R diagram of Figure 16-1A, with another ten Dow Jones Industrials. At the

Figure 20-6: Control model 20-2 superimposed on O/R diagram 16-1C

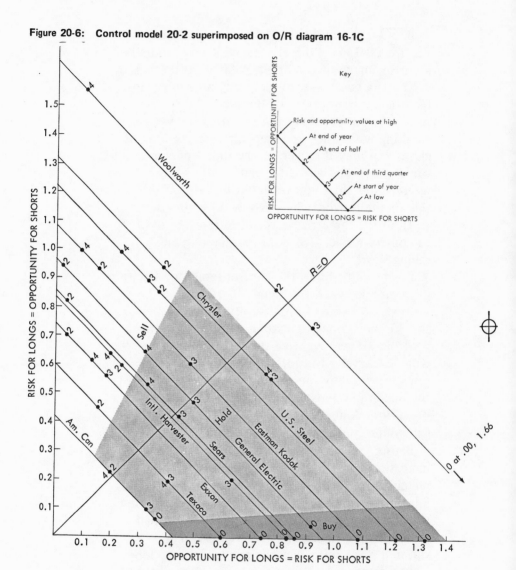

Figure 20-7: Control model 20-3 superimposed on O/R diagram 16-1A

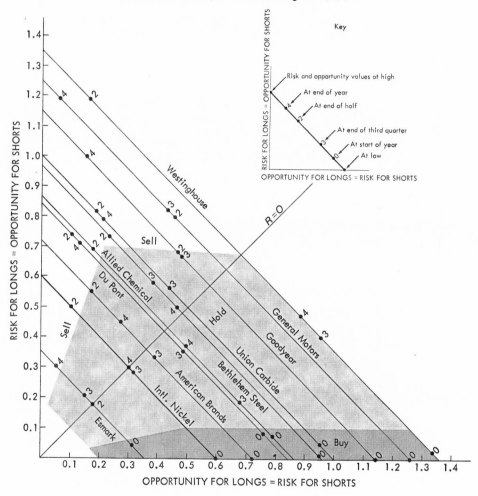

start of the year (which was loaded with buying
opportunity at that point) all ten stocks, from
Westinghouse to Esmark, were priced low enough
to lie within the buy area, and four of those lay

right on the zero-risk line. By midyear, price increases had driven seven of the ten through the hold areas and the sell lines. Two more stocks, American Brands and Goodyear, were nudging sell points. Only Esmark, the least volatile of the ten, was sluggish.

By the end of the third quarter, five of the ten stocks had retreated below the risk-equals-opportunity line, giving further evidence of the wisdom of taking profits under conservative sell criteria.

In Figure 20-8, the short-selling control model of Figure 20-5 has been superimposed on the ten Dow Jones stocks of Figure 16-1B. We see that at the start of the year, when prices were at or near their lows, there were no good short sales. However, at their subsequent highs, all ten were *possible* short sales, depending upon new forward assessments made at the times that the high prices were reached. Even without such reassessment, though, we can see that four stocks lay in the sell-short area at the end of the half. Of these, American Telephone and Procter & Gamble, had retreated through the hold-short area and beyond the short-cover line by the end of the third quarter. By the same time, Johns-Manville, another early gainer, had retreated to its low for the year. The substantial profits to be made by shorting such stocks under favorable conditions of risk and opportunity are evident.

Now the time has come for you, the reader, to start building your own control models. We suggest that you begin by using tracing paper to place over the three O/R diagrams of Chapter 16, which describe the action of the 30 Dow Jones

Figure 20-8: Control model 20-5 superimposed on O/R diagram 16-1B

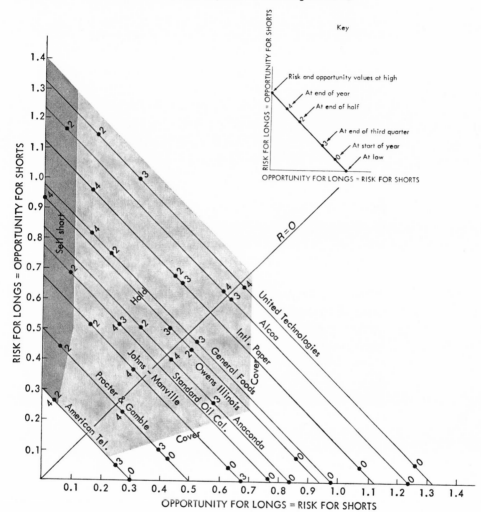

Industrials over a one-year time span, super-
imposing your own buy, hold, and sell criteria.

Next, using graph paper, draw O/R diagrams
for stocks of your choice, and test how your
control models would have worked during past
time periods (annually, say). Use the appropriate
formulas to determine volatility, risk, opportunity,
and timing criteria, with calculations based on
historical highs and lows, and current price at the
start of the period selected.

Finally, repeat the process using now-current
prices and estimated future highs and lows—and
you're on your own!

Remember, every stock whose characteristic
volatility line traverses the buy and hold areas of
any well-made control model is confined to its
own volatility trap (Chapter 10), so by tracking it
(Chapters 11 and 12) and following the steps of
efficient portfolio management (Chapter 19),
superior performance must result—a wondrous
feat indeed!

Index

INDEX

A-B

Astrologers, 47
Barron's, 12, 133
Beta coefficient, 18-19, 100-102; *see also* Poor Boy beta
Buying; *see* Buying long
Buying long, 5-6, 9-10, 12-13, 20, 65-66; *see also* Control
    models; Opportunity; Risk; *and* Tracking price

C

Chartists, 45-48
Commerce, U.S. Department of, 48
Comovement with the market, 19, 100-102; *see also* Beta
    coefficient *and* Swinging with the market
Comparison, screening, selection, 140-41
Control models, 42, 57, 59, 93, 119, 145-58; *see also*
    Efficient portfolio, management *and* Timing
Council of Economic Advisers, 13, 47
Current price factor, 30-31, 34-35; *see also* Opportunity
    and Risk

D

Dividends and interest, 10, 20
    effect on risk and opportunity, 35-36
Douglas Aircraft, 4
Dow Jones Industrials, 77, 93-95, 99, 101-2, 115-19, 153-58
Du Pont, 93-94

E

Economists, 46-48
Efficient market, 18; *see also* Random Walk theory
Efficient portfolio
    definition, 139
    management, 139-41, 158
Errors in forecasting, 73-74, 88, 107-11, 151

F-G

Forecasting highs and lows, 91-96, 99-103, 115; *see also*
    Errors in forecasting
Great Crash, 3, 11

U-Z

Uptick, 11, 13
Value Line, 93-94
Volatility, 18, 57-58; *see also* Control models; Errors in
forecasting; Price, price fluctuations; Swinging with
the market; *and* Tracking price
line, 63-65, 108-11, 158
measurement, 29-32, 63-65, 77, 101
trap, 69-74, 77-82, 85-88, 119, 153
Zero-plus tick, 11